Henry Blackburn

English art in 1884, illustrated by facsimile sketches by the artists

Henry Blackburn

English art in 1884, illustrated by facsimile sketches by the artists

ISBN/EAN: 9783742891709

Manufactured in Europe, USA, Canada, Australia, Japa

Cover: Foto ©Thomas Meinert / pixelio.de

Manufactured and distributed by brebook publishing software
(www.brebook.com)

Henry Blackburn

English art in 1884, illustrated by facsimile sketches by the artists

English Art

IN

1884

ILLUSTRATED

BY FACSIMILE SKETCHES BY THE ARTISTS.

AND FOURTEEN FULL-PAGE PHOTO-ENGRAVINGS

EDITED BY

HENRY BLACKBURN

EDITOR OF "ACADEMY NOTES;" LECTURER ON ART; AUTHOR OF "BRETON FOLK;" "NORMANDY PICTURESQUE;"
"ARTISTS AND ARABS," ETC.

NEW YORK
D. APPLETON AND COMPANY
I, 3, AND 5 BOND STREET
1885

No. 389. *"The Herring-Market at Sea."* COLIN HUNTER.

PREFACE.

THE art of England, as represented in painting, water-colors, and sculpture, is so full of activity and resource, that it has been thought desirable to gather into one compendious volume an indication of the work of a year.

In the galleries containing new pictures, there have been exhibited in London alone, during the past year, upward of five thousand works. Of these, nearly four hundred are sketched in this volume, generally by the artists themselves. They have been selected from the exhibitions of the Royal Academy, the Grosvenor Gallery, the Institute of Oil-Painters, and the Water-Color Societies. Should the plan be pursued another year, other galleries will be included.

The majority of English pictures pass annually into private hands, and the American public would hardly be aware of their existence,

were it not for the publication of engravings and etchings. But no
engravings or etchings could keep pace with the art activity of England,* and it became necessary to devise some simple means of presenting to the public an indication, or outline, of the art of the year.

It is maintained by some writers that the English school of painting is, at the present time, the first in the world; that there is a
wider measure of success among its foremost men, and more individuality and interest in the work of the younger, than in any other
school. Certainly, as regards portraiture, the country of Gainsborough
and Reynolds would seem to be again first in the field; and, in landscape, the country of Turner and David Cox is producing work from
which foreign countries derive much of their inspiration.

It is not the purpose of this publication, which should be more
descriptive than critical, to discuss the comparative merits of modern
schools, but rather to direct attention to a powerful factor in "the
year's art."

The English figure-painters, headed by such artists as Sir Frederick
Leighton, President of the Royal Academy, E. Burne-Jones, J. E.
Millais, Holman Hunt, G. F. Watts, L. Alma-Tadema, E. J. Poynter,
and others, are producing work equal to any period in the history of
art. As compared with the Paris *Salon*, there have been few large
and important pictures exhibited; but, on the other hand, it would
be difficult to point to greater technical successes, or to modern paintings on which more skill, labor, and cultivation, had been bestowed,
than on the "*Cymon and Iphigenia*" (page 2), by Sir Frederick Leighton; the "*Hadrian in Britain*" (page 4), by L. Alma-Tadema; or the

---

The number of pictures sent in to the Royal Academy alone last spring was eight thousand and
— — — eighteen hundred and fifty six were exhibited.

"*King Cophetua*" (page 141), by Burne-Jones. Mr. Holman Hunt has been engaged for five years on one picture, and Mr. G. F. Watts and Mr. E. J. Poynter have contributed little to the year's exhibitions; the latter having been engaged, with Sir Frederick Leighton, on designs for the decoration of St. Paul's Cathedral in London.

The influence of such artists and the teaching in our schools have raised the standard in drawing and composition in a remarkable manner during the last few years. But variety of character and individuality are still the marked characteristics of English work, students in England being less influenced by any master's style than in the *ateliers* of Paris or Munich.

In landscape it will be observed that English artists are not occupied in composing pictures like Turner or Claude; they are followers rather of that school of landscape-painting which found its best expression in the work of Constable and Crowe, and, in pure water-colors, in the drawings of David Cox and Dewint. The sentiment of landscape is less considered than quality and truth to nature.

Thus, without entering into a discussion of comparative merits, it may be pointed out that the art of England has qualities and characteristics which should be more widely known; and when the great barriers against progress—protective tariffs—shall be broken down, a knowledge of English art may become as wide-spread as that of its literature, and a love for it be as deeply implanted in American soil.

The notice of the Water-Color Societies will be interesting in connection with the proposed exhibition by English water-color artists, to be held in New York and at the Museum of Fine Arts, Boston, in 1885. The works of many artists spoken of here, and whose sketches appear on these pages, will then be seen for the first time in America.

Of the *illustrations* in "English Art" a few words must be said. When, just ten years ago, the possibility of obtaining an exact facsimile of an artist's pen-drawing on a "relief"-block, to print with the type, was first practically demonstrated, it opened out a wide field of interest and usefulness. By means of the invention of photo-mechanical engraving we are enabled to present to the reader of these pages the very hand-work of the artist side by side with the text. The communication between the artist and the public has thus become very rapid and direct. The artist, having completed his picture, puts down on paper, in the fewest lines, the leading features or accents of it; this memorandum or sketch is reproduced without the aid of the wood-engraver, and, by means of the printing-press, multiplied over the world. There is no attempt, or should be no attempt, at making a finished picture; the object is to indicate, in the fewest lines and in the most direct way, what the artist had in his mind. To some artists this power is given in an exceptional degree. Sir John Gilbert, the veteran illustrator, in his sketch, on page 16, of the weary horseman on the morning of the battle of Agincourt, indicates exactly the character and composition of his picture. More subtly expressed in these pages—so tenderly, indeed, that we wonder at the power which conveys an impression by such simple means—is the disturbed little face in Marcus Stone's painting entitled "*Fallen out*," on page 21. No elaborate wood-engraving would have done this for us on the small scale necessary. Again, Mr. Eyre Crowe, in the sketch of his picture of the little scholars at St. Maclou, Rouen (page 23), tells the public what he saw as clearly as in the painting. And in many other figure-subjects the story is told by this process in a very few lines indeed.

In portraiture, illustrations are of necessity less interesting, but the sketch on page 155, of Millais's portrait of Lord Lorne, from the Grosvenor Gallery, gives the character of it exactly, and it is the style of a portrait we seek to know.

In landscape we may often obtain an accurate idea not only of the composition, but of the sentiment of a picture, as, for instance, of the quietness in Mr. Parton's autumn scene, " *The Vale of Light,*" sketched on page 97, and of the wind in the trees in " *A Wintry Dirge* " (page 103), by Alfred East.

This system of expression, of communication between two minds by means of a few touches, is the great art of the illustrator. It has been shown in a high degree in the war sketches by Detaille in Parisian newspapers.

But the tendency of all illustrators is to elaborate, and the fashion tends toward smooth and highly-finished illustrations everywhere. Even the French artists, imitating the English system of making sketches of their pictures exhibited in the *Salon,* tend to over-elaboration. In engravings of pictures there is generally too much given, and a picture is presented to us which is far from the original. The most attractive reproduction is often one from which the individuality of the originator has passed away. In sketching a picture, the great art is " *the art of leaving out,*" and, looking to the future, it would be well for young artists to make a study of expressing effects in the fewest lines. In this method of work we are approaching nearer in artistic value to the reproductions of drawings by Mantegna and Dürer, and to the etchings by Rembrandt ; the value of the new system, as compared with the old, being in the almost illimitable number of copies that may now be printed from a single block.

b

The *full-page plates* in this volume have been photographed direct from the painting, and reproduced by a system of photo-engraving; but photographs of pictures, valuable and interesting as they are, are very far from giving the true balance of color of the original. In the reproduction of many compositions photography is of the utmost value; but the light on the sea in Colin Hunter's "*Herring-Market,*" which we give at the head of this Preface, could not have been indicated without lines. In short, we are still far from the possibility of reproducing a picture satisfactorily without the hand-work of the artist on the reproduction.

In turning over a portfolio of engravings or etchings, or an ordinary illustrated book, we may linger admiringly on the perfection of the engraver's art; but in this volume we should care as little for the *method* of reproducing an artist's sketch as for character in the handwriting of a telegram.

Thus regarded, "English Art in 1884" will be found of great interest in drawing attention to the work of many artists whose pictures, from various causes, have never been illustrated before. And the possessor of this book will be a collector of autographs which will increase in interest year by year; for never, we believe, in the history of art has one volume contained the hand-work of so many different men.

HENRY BLACKBURN.

163 VICTORIA STREET, WESTMINSTER,
August 1, 1884.

₄ In the production of this volume I have to acknowledge the kind assistance of Mr. M. Phipps-Jackson and Mr. Frederick Wedmore. The illustrations are by various processes, English, French, and American. A number of the blocks are by the Lefman process, from a work entitled "The Royal Academy Illustrated."

No. 986. *"Water-Lilies and Poppies."* W. J. MUCKLEY.

No. 232. "Victory." Thomas Blinks.

77 × 48.

CONTENTS.

No. 765. "Disputed Possession." W. B. Baird.

LIST OF FULL-PAGE PHOTO-ENGRAVINGS.

₊ For Engravings in the text, see Index to Artists, at the end of the volume.

THE ROYAL ACADEMY.

THE one hundred and sixteenth exhibition of the Royal Academy of Arts, at Burlington House, in London, contained eighteen hundred and fifty-six works of art in painting in oils and water-colors, engraving, etching, architectural designs, and sculpture.

There are nine rooms devoted to oil-paintings, of which the principal is the fine long Gallery III, where the banquets and other meetings are held, and where the president addresses the students at the annual giving of prizes.

No. 340. *"Night."* P. H. CALDERON, R. A.*
"Empress of silence and queen of sleep."

In this gallery the principal pictures of the year (works of members of the Academy, of whom there are forty, with a right to exhibit eight pictures each) are generally to be found on the line.

Let us look first at the prominent features of this gallery. In the place of honor, in the center of the north wall, was a large picture by Sir Frederick Leighton, the president, a work upon which he has been long engaged, and upon the studies and models for which much has been written. It is by no means the most successful work of the painter, and interests us less than many earlier paintings—such as the *"Daphneforia,"* of 1876, and his graceful picture of *"Wedded,"* exhibited two years ago.

The painting of *"Cymon and Iphigenia"* is refined and scholarly; the subject grandly and (as we see in the outline) conventionally and decora-

---

* The figures below the illustrations indicate the sizes of the pictures. The numbers are those of the official catalogues of the various public galleries where the pictures have been exhibited.

tively treated; elaborate and highly finished, rich in color, and almost perfect in the drawing and arrangement of draperies.

It is Boccaccio's rendering of the familiar story of Cymon and Iphigenia that the president has chosen for his theme. The scene is on the edge of a wood in the Island of Cyprus, where, "under the breath of a May night, is seen asleep a lovely lady, clad only in her subtile vesture, and with no guards excepting two sleeping attendants and a little child."

NO. 278.　"*Cymon and Iphigenia.*"　SIR FREDERICK LEIGHTON, P. R. A.

Near stands Cymon, the young peasant, transfixed by the sight of her beauty. To depict the gradual awakening of better thoughts and a higher life in an uneducated peasant, under the influence of Iphigenia's charms, has been the great effort of the painter—the refining influence of art upon the uncultivated being the moral of the story. In the absence of many pictures of high aim or intention, and considering the great want of thoroughness in modern work, this painting sets an example to students. The photogravure produced by Messrs. Goupil will give a good indication of the design. Sir Frederick Leighton takes much interest in this new and wonderful method of reproduction.

Opposite to the foregoing is the principal contribution by J. E. Millais, R. A., a picture of five figures, for which the sum of twenty-five thousand dollars has been paid. The painter of a long line of celebrated pictures—of "*The Huguenots,*" of "*The Gambler's Wife,*" of "*Autumn Leaves,*" of "*The Yeoman of the Guard*"; the greatest living portrait-painter, and, we might almost add, the greatest landscape-painter—has given us this year one subject-picture, lacking, it is true, the absorbing human interest of many of his former works, but bearing the mark of genius upon it as unmistakably as its predecessors.

The scene is a wood by a cool rivulet—the period soon after the battle of Culloden—where three Scotch lasses are seated, listening to an English fifer-boy—who has come north with the troops—the latter clad in the crude-colored red-and-yellow uniform with white gaiters depicted in Hogarth's "*March to Finchley.*" The interest centers, we might say culminates, in the figure of the boy playing, which is almost as powerful, as a character-study, as the old "*Yeoman of the Guard,*" painted in 1877. It has been suggested that the boy-figure might with advantage have made one picture, and the three girls another. For the sake of harmony and "keeping," this change might have been made with advan-

No. 347. "*An Idyll,* 1745." J. E. MILLAIS, R. A.

tage, for the crudeness of the uniform, red, yellow, and white, the painter has rendered with such uncompromising force as seriously to detract from the beauty of the children, and to take our attention from the rich quality of much of the work. The painting has the peculiar charm which pervades all Millais's representations of children, and the composition is well indicated in the rough sketch.

At the head of this gallery, in the center of the wall, was a large picture by L. Alma-Tadema, R.A. This painter has produced nothing so important in size or composition since "*The Picture-Gallery*" and "*The Sculpture-Gallery,*" which were exhibited in the Academy in 1874 and 1875, and are now in Mr. Gambart's villa at Nice. "*The Pottery*" is in some sense a pendant to the foregoing. It represents the visit of the Emperor Hadrian, with his wife and attendants, to a Romano-British pottery. The following description, from details communicated by the artist to the correspondent of a London newspaper, will be read with interest in connection with the outline on page 4:

"The exact locality of the manufactory is not signaled. We may suppose it to have been situated in the center of one of the great Roman colonies, and to have possessed show-rooms in which not merely the local ware, but specimens from all the famous kilns, could be inspected. We are not allowed to decide which of all the sorts presented to the emperor is actually being made by the fair-haired artisans whom we see at work, under the archway of the staircase. Upon the stairs itself two half-naked men, girt with broad leather pots are carrying specimen-trays up to the emperor. In the tray of the first of these, whose entire figure is seen on the right of the composition, the peculiar drab pots made in the Upchurch marshes are presented to us; while the man who follows him, and whose head and uplifted hands alone are visible, bears aloft a tray of nothing but the slate-colored

No. 245. "*Hadrian in Britain: visiting a Romano-British Pottery.*" L. ALMA-TADEMA, R.A.

Durobrivian-ware, which was made round Castor, in the valley of the Nen in Northamptonshire.

"At the top of the staircase we see an open gallery filled with the distinguished Roman visitors. Hadrian himself, in a purple toga, stands at the head of the stairs, examining a vase with an expression of dignified affability. The master-potter leans forward in the act of explanation, and we see his light red hair and beard in contrast to the black hair of all the Romans. Behind Hadrian stands his friend Lucius Verus, afterward father to the Emperor Commodus. He is in attendance on Hadrian, and keeps the rest of the suite a little in the background. He leans with a dandified air on a long staff, which is tipped with a little Venus carved in ivory. On the other side of the gallery the great ladies cluster round the potter's wife. She is represented as a blonde girl, of extremely fair skin, in a pale-blue dress; her back is turned to us, and we can only judge of her beauty from the delicacy of her neck and shoulders. Mr. Alma-Tadema declares that he turned her face away because he despaired of doing justice to her fresh English beauty. She is talking to the Empress Sabina, Hadrian's wife, a dignified Roman matron, and to Balbilla, the friend of Sabina, the famous female wit whose Bœotian verses were inscribed by Hadrian's command on the base of the Vocal Memnon. Between the groups there leans over the stair-case, in a lilac toga, Servianus, Hadrian's sister's husband.

"The accessories of this interesting group of historical personages are full of ingenuity and suggestiveness, as always in Mr. Alma-Tadema's pictures. The architecture is rough, in red terra-cotta, which has been made on the premises; for the master-potter, like a Doulton of to-day, makes at the same time the roughest things for practical uses, and the most delicate for ornamental uses. At the elbow of the staircase stands a beautiful black vase, which is a careful reproduction of the famous Colchester Pot, which was discovered in 1853; this has interesting reliefs running round it as a frieze. Another large and graceful vase is full of wall-flowers, and a great wreath of primroses is wound around it to show at what time of the year Hadrian's visit was made. The wall of the staircase is copied from a mosaic found on the floors of the famous Roman villa of Bignor, near Arundel, and Mr. Alma-Tadema considers that such walls and pavements as this made in mosaic would probably be manufactured at such a pottery as he has painted. the *tessalæ* being of terra-cotta and local stone. In the corner of the staircase, near the center of the picture, we see one of those interesting little bits of reproduction of antique life in which Mr. Alma-Tadema is so eminently happy. This is the altar of the household god. A snake is painted round it, and by a little lamp there is placed a votive offering of onions, sacred to the Penates. The potters have painted this inscription as a welcome to their emperor :

'Ave Imperator Cæsar
Divi Trajani parth. filius
Divi Nervæ nepos
Trajanus Hadrianus
Locupletator Orbis.'

Hadrian was not, indeed, declared _Aσυρλετατωρ_ by the senate till after the date of this picture, but Mr. Alma-Tadema thinks that it would probably be in some grateful colony that the title would first be, unofficially, suggested.

"The painter possesses a unique collection of drawings of the Romano-British pottery, and he has visited most of the museums, and particularly those at Colchester, Maidstone, and Cirencester, to make studies for this picture."

As a work of art, probably no painting has given the artist more labor, but the result as a whole can hardly be considered an artistic success. There is nothing in this large picture to equal in quality or charm "_The Oleander_" of last year. The design of "_The Pottery_" is complicated, and seems to transgress many of the ordinary rules of composition, but the painting of the man's figure ascending the stairs has hardly been surpassed in any period of art; certainly there was nothing to approach it, technically, in this year's exhibition. Some details also are painted in Mr. Alma-Tadema's best and strongest manner, but as a whole the picture fails—the effect of perspective is questionable, the great blank wall in the middle of the canvas is uninteresting, and the cutting off of the head of the lower figure carrying pots is unpleasing. We are made to care most for details, for the painting of flesh, for the texture of Hadrian's robe, and for the draperies and ornaments of the women. Thus, we might sum up Mr. Alma-Tadema's art, as shown in this picture, as _devotion to accessories_, to technical triumphs of a high order. But Mr. Alma-Tadema, like Mr. Millais, is also great in portraiture, especially in the portraits of his friends. These were exhibited in the Grosvenor Gallery in 1884.

The "picture of the year," that is to say, the picture upon which more has been said and written than any other, is Mr. Orchardson's "_Mariage de Convenance_." The three figures which we see in the sketch, in a curiously-empty apartment, have set half London talking during the month of May. The painter of Napoleon in 1880, and Voltaire in 1883, has achieved an extraordinary success in his "_Mariage de Convenance_." The figures (the lady in white-satin dress) are seen under a glow of subdued light from the colored lamp over the dinner-table; the distribution of light and shade is very harmonious, and the management of color on the table laden with fruit most skillful. But the interest of the picture to the majority has been, so to speak, more literary than artistic; it is the story, not altogether a pleasant one, that absorbs attention.

Mr. George Augustus Sala, a great admirer of Mr. Orchardson's work, writes thus on the "_Mariage de Convenance_": "We are in the dining-room of a fashionable mansion, and Beatrice and Benedick have been dining _en petite comité_. Dinner is over, dessert is being served and the pair are being waited upon by a judicious butler. Beatrice is young, comely, and fully aware of her comeliness, and she is dressed in the strictest accordance with the latest behests of the 'Ladies' Gazette of Fashion.' Anon, you think, the brougham will be in attendance, the *grande dame de par le monde* will be carefully shawled and cloaked, and the loving couple will honor a box at the opera or a stall at the Haymarket with their presence. But are they a loving couple? Alas and alack! although Beatrice is youthful and fair and fascinating, Benedick is old—and not venerable. His valet has made the best of his master's sparse locks and grizzled mustache; but he is beyond the help of valets, and even of the magician Truefitt himself. An excellent old gentleman, no doubt. Although he feebly wags his head over the glass which the butler is replenishing, he is evidently, as regards breeding, very high. A baronet probably; member for his county

41 × 60.

No. 341. *"Mariage de Convenance."* W. Q. ORCHARDSON, R. A.

possibly; evidently wealthy. Fond of antique silver, old books, old illuminated manuscripts. Well known at Christie's; a member of several Pall Mall clubs. He grudges Beatrice nor diamonds, nor dresses from Worth, nor point-lace from Élise, nor bonnets from Louise, nor horses and carriages and Dutch pugs, nor trips to Nice or the Engadine—and it is a '*Mariage de Convenance.*'

"Only three personages in this domestic drama of fashionable life? Why, the imagination at once fills the dining-room, the servants' hall, the whole house with people knowing a variety of things, occult and awful. The brougham is driving up to the door of the great mansion; but it is Black Care and not the groom who sits by the coachman's side.

At one end of the splendid dining-room table, laden with costly plate, with choice flowers and luscious fruit, covers Calmcity, humbled, vainly trying to preserve its dignity, laboriously endeavoring to put a good face upon things, but hopelessly drifting into Fogyism, utterly unable to accept the situation, and ashamed of being old. In the shadows behind Benedick's chair seem to hover 'the Painful Family of Death, more hideous than their concern' the ills that rack the joints or fire the veins, that strain every laboring sinew or in the deeper vitals rage. And at the other end of the table—a wide, wide gulf, not only of fruit and flower-decked damask napery, but of years, and imperfect sympathies, and unimparted thoughts and blasted hopes yawning between them—sits Beatrice, young, beautiful, shapely, vascular, and in a silent, mad rage. She looks as though on but slight provocation she would tear her rich raiment from her shoulders, and wrench her rings from her fingers and her bracelets from her wrists, and fling the gewgaws at the head of her husband or of the judicious butler.

"In the *Mariage de Convenance*, the handsome, willful, self-tormenting Beatrice, the effete and dispirited but always high-toned and high-bred Benedick, and the judicious butler, who is so careful in whispering the precise date of the vintage of the Château Margaux, and is aware, besides, of such an alarming variety of things, are all adequately modeled, or, to speak more technically, 'made out,' with due attention to the laws of convexity and concavity. Of the wealth and subtilty of expression in the faces of the three personages enough has been said in sketching the wholly imaginary drama in which they are taking part."

Columns have been written in this strain, an extract from which may prove more interesting than dwelling entirely on the technical merits of this picture. Mr. Orchardson ranks high as a painter of *genre*, but, to get a more complete idea of his style and method, his smaller picture of "*The Farmer's Daughter*," in the Grosvenor Gallery this year, should be looked at in the section devoted to that gallery.

"*The Toast of the Kitcat Club*," as presented to us by Mr. W. F. Yeames, R. A., is more interesting historically than for any special quality in the painting. In Mr. Orchardson's work there is much that is subtile and suggestive; here in Mr. Yeames's picture, which hangs beside it, all is careful, literal, and, as far as possible, matter of fact.

The members of the literary clubs in the last century were intimately associated with the society of the time, and there is nothing doubtful in the story that the little Lady Mary Pierrepont was brought in to be admired and "kissed all round!" The Whig gentlemen, we read, drank her health upstanding, gave her sweetmeats, and had her name cut on a drinking-glass in honor of her visit. "Never," writes Lady Mary Wortley Montagu, "did I pass so happy an evening." Mr. Yeames has labored hard to give the portraits and costumes from the best authorities. Sir Godfrey Kneller is in the foreground; next to him Garth; Congreve turning in his chair; Tonson, the publisher; above him, Addison; and Steele, with a wine-glass in his hand. Marlborough and others on the left of the picture. Altogether, in the lack of historic painting, of the first class, we are glad to welcome Mr. Yeames's work, and to reproduce it in our record of "English Art in 1884."

45 × 39.

No. 332. "*The Toast of the Kitcat Club.*" W. F. YEAMES, R. A.

"It having fallen to the turn of the Duke of Kingston to propose a beauty as the annual toast of the club, he nominated his little daughter Lady Mary Pierrepont (afterward Lady Mary Wortley Montagu). Some of the members demurred, as they had not seen her. The duke sent for her, and when she arrived she was received with acclamation, her claims unanimously allowed, and she was petted and caressed by all the eminent men present."

Mr. Philip Calderon, R. A., is represented in his principal work by a single figure of "*Night*," which is sketched at the head of this chapter. Always with grace and refinement, as distinctive characteristics of his art, Mr. Calderon, when at his best, rises to the rank of those masters who, with poetic conception of a high order, have combined great technical

2

This realization of his present subject is the life-size figure of a Greek girl resting on a marble seat, with the starlighted canopy of heaven above her, and in the distance Corinth, or some other city of Greece. The principal motive of the
image repeats, whether in sentiment, color, or line. The deep-blue sky, the girl's seated
figure, the upper half of which is draped in white, with dark-blue robe across her knees,
the marble balustrade, altogether form a fine and harmonious picture. This, and another,
entitled "*Poet*," are to form part of the decoration of a dining-room in the house of a well-
known art-collector in London.

Mr. J. C. Horsley, one of the elder of the Royal Academicians, sends a picture of a
country churchyard, with children and sheep that have strayed among the tombstones — a
familiar enough subject in England,
treated with simplicity and truth in
all details. The large, heavy stone
slabs, now almost discarded in England, the pretty lych-gate under the
yew-tree, the group at the church-
porch—are all portraits, so to speak.
A homely picture, without any special
quality in the painting, of which a
writer remarks: "We have not the
slightest doubt that Mr. Horsley saw
what is here represented, for no artist
would manufacture such a scene for
himself. The pretty children, with the
glory of their young life fresh upon them, heedlessly hiding over the dead, who once probably had done in like mirth what these little ones are doing—the pastor and his flock, nay,
even the animals, the sheep, suggesting memorable words once spoken—everything introduced into the scene carries out, not without an occasional touch of pathos, the simple
story of life and death the artist seeks to convey."

One of the largest pictures in the Royal Academy is Mr. Goodall's picture of "*The
Flight into Egypt*," which faces the spectator as he enters the galleries. It is a powerful
painting, much darker in tone than would appear from the sketch. The Pyramids have
been painted often, and "*The Flight into Egypt*" is no new subject for the artist; but
Mr. Goodall's skill and knowledge of Eastern atmospheric effects endow the subject with
new interest. In the absence of almost all religious subjects in the Academy, this picture
is welcome to many. Another large picture by the same artist is called "*A New Light*

No. 272. "*Hide and Seek*." J. C. HORSLEY, R.A.

16 × 61.

in the Harem," depicting a young mother and child in an Eastern interior, with a Nubian nurse. This work is rich in color and costume, and full of character and vivacity. Mr. Goodall, like Mr. Edwin Long, R. A., has made his greatest success by the painting of single

No. 619. "*The Flight into Egypt.*" F. GOODALL, R. A.

figures from scriptural subjects, figures many of which are familiar to us in engravings. Both artists are celebrated for the painting of ornaments and draperies glowing in sunlight.

Mr. Edwin Long reserves his large works for private exhibition; the figure he has chosen for his principal Academy picture is that of "*Thisbe.*" It is related by Ovid that, during the celebration of the festival of Bacchus, the daughters of Minyas preferred staying at home, rather than take part in what they regarded as impious rites, and, in order that time might pass pleasantly, one of them proposed to tell a story. The first story related was that of Pyramus and Thisbe. Pyramus is described as the most beauteous of youths, and Thisbe as "preferred before all the damsels that the East contained." Living in adjoining houses, they became acquainted, and mutually enamoured of each other, and would have united themselves in marriage, but their fathers forbade it. But they managed, however, to communicate by nods and signs. Afterward they discovered a crack through the party-wall that divided their two houses, through which they were able to converse, Thisbe on one side and Pyramus on the other. This is the passage in the poem, and the incident that Mr. Edwin Long has chosen for his Royal Academy picture. The artist has borne well in mind the poet's brief description of Thisbe's charms—he tells us that she was "preferred

Is for all other damsels that the East contained"—the modeling of the figure, that of a young woman, not a girl, listening with rapt attention to the accents of her lover as they reach her through the chink in the wall, is indicated in the sketch. The attitude is easy, natural, and graceful, and the expression modest yet fervent. This picture has been reproduced in pure line-engraving by Monsieur G. Bertinos.

No. 353, *"Cruel Necessity,"* by W. P. Frith, R.A. The artist here illustrates a story told of the Protector Cromwell, that he visited the Banqueting-House, Whitehall, where the body of that hapless monarch, Charles I, was laid the night succeeding his execution, and, quietly ascending the stairs, he gazed at the king's remains for some time, giving utterance to the suggestive words referred to in the title of the picture. With the political aspect of the question we have really nothing whatever to do; but there is something singularly solemn in the idea of the great man who, in the plenitude of his power and in cold blood, had upset the government of a powerful nation and brought its ruler to the block, feeling impelled to secretly view the remains of the man whose life he had just taken away. Two Cavaliers, Lord Southampton and another, are said to

56 × 33.

No. 358.   *"Think."*   F. Leroi, R.A.

"An envious wall the Babylonian maid
From Pyramus, her gentle lover, stayed.
Yet here a tiny chink none else had seen
Some of so long lent's messages between.
They kissed its stony mouth like lovers true,
But neither side would let the kisses through."
     OVID, *Met. IV,* 55 *et seq.*

have witnessed the extraordinary occurrence. History appears to point to the fact that the persistence of the king in a wrong-headed and perverse course had resulted in a state of things where either his life, or that of his sworn opponent, Cromwell, must be sacrificed.

No. 306, *"Dr. Johnson and Mrs. Siddons,"* is a work by the same well-known artist. The fascinating actress, Mrs. Siddons, was, it appears, in the habit of visiting Dr. Johnson constantly, not long before his death. Our great lexicographer, who was scarcely noted for urbanity, was, however, generally polite to the fair sex, and, although himself so distinguished a man of letters, he acknowledged with graceful courtesy and gratitude the attention of a lady who was in every way an ornament to histrionic art. These visits, which took place in 1784, shortly before the doctor's death, in his sixty-fifth year, found him so infirm that he was unable to accompany the fair actress to her carriage, but he was wont to thank her with a high-bred politeness, and in a set formulary of words he never varied.

Mr. W. P. Frith, the painter of the "*Derby Day*" (so popular in the Royal Academy in 1858, and now in the National Gallery) and other similar works, has given us nothing so interesting for some years as this portrait-picture of Dr. Johnson and Mrs. Siddons, of which we give a full-page illustration.

No. 353. "*Cruel Necessity.*" W. P. FRITH, R.A.

"The night after King Charles I was beheaded, my Lord Southampton and a friend got leave to sit up by the body in the Banqueting-House at Whitehall. As they were sitting there very melancholy at about two o'clock in the morning, they heard the tread of somebody coming slowly up the stairs. By-and-by the door opened and a man entered, very much muffled up in his cloak. He approached the body, considered it very attentively for some time, and then shook his head and sighed out the words, 'Cruel necessity.' He then departed in the same slow and concealed manner as he had come in. Lord Southampton used to say that he could not distinguish anything of his face, but that by his voice and gait he took him to be Oliver Cromwell."

No. 463. "*Faith,*" by Edward Armitage, R.A., is a scriptural design, showing the Saviour, while walking through the streets with his disciples, followed by a crowd of the poor and of those who believed in his sacred mission. Some of these—sick, blind, and in sorry plight—have hope in their hearts that, if Christ only wills it, they may be healed. One poor woman, strong in faith, feels assured her cure is certain, if she can but kiss the hem of the Saviour's garment. And it is recorded in Holy Writ that Christ turned himself about, "feeling that virtue had gone out of him," and the trusting sufferer was made whole. The chief figure in this fine group is instinct with calm, grand dignity—the crowd typifying those who in this world watch, and wait, and suffer.

Mr. Armitage was born in London, in 1817, and was a pupil of Paul Delaroche.

This artist, and Mr. J. R. Herbert, R. A., are among the few exponents of sacred art among members of the Royal Academy at the present time. Mr. Herbert, who is the painter of the celebrated picture in the Houses of Parliament of "*Moses with the Tables of the Law*," still contributes to the Academy, but his day is past, and his pictures can hardly be regarded seriously by the critic. Mr. Armitage still holds his position, and in choice of historic subjects sets a good example to younger men. Mr. Armitage's lectures before the students at the Academy have lately been published, and are well worth reading.

38 x 29.

No. 292. "*The Angler's Rest.*" H. S. MARKS, R. A.

No. 383. "*The Pet Plant,*" by H. Stacy Marks, R. A., is one of the studies of monkish character which the artist peculiarly affects, and which, it is needless to add, he executes exceedingly well. A good father, whose duty is evidently that of gardener, combined with his more spiritual office, is in the conservatory of the monastery, attending to the plants. Pets, it is to be presumed, are scarcely an allowable luxury with priests, but this worthy

DR. JOHNSON AND MRS. SIDDONS.
W. P. FRITH, R.A.

man has transgressed the law in as permissible a manner as possible when, yielding to temptation, he makes a pet of a flower.

Another single-figure study of a monk, No. 45, "*The Stopped Key,*" by Mr. Marks, represents a priest at the monastery-door with a basket of comestibles at his side which he has just brought from a neighboring village. The old fellow is trying to pick out something from his key, which will not turn in the lock. This picture is very similar in style and composition to "*The Pet Plant.*"

More important and interesting than either of the former is No. 292, "*The Angler's Rest,*" by the same hand. A piscator, in costume of about a century ago, is seated outside a picturesque-looking country inn, chatting to some traveler. Sportsmen are impracticable creatures for general social purposes, their conversation being, as a rule, limited to their sport. One of the characters Mr. Marks delineates is evidently holding forth with much emphasis upon the delights of some past great day's sport, or of the best method, under certain circumstances, of ensnaring the finny tribe. In the distance, a peep of bright, flat lands, with a winding stream, forms an attractive background. Many accurately studied details are worth noting, such as the timbers of "The Dolphin Inn," the traveler's old-fash-

ioned seat by the road-side, the costumes, the cat, the pigeons, and the general *quiet* of a scene soon to disappear from England before railway-hotels.

No. 359, "*The Vigil,*" by John Pettie, R. A. The artist takes us back to the ages of chivalry in this subject. A young esquire is here represented kneeling upon the stone floor of a chapel, watching his armor, and this he will have to do the whole night through, until the succeeding day sees him entitled to the honor of knight-

4b x 6b.

No. 359. "*The Vigil.*" John Pettie, R. A.
(*Chantry Fund.*)

hood. The cold, gray light of early dawn strikes upon the young man, who wears a white garb and crimson mantle, and he fixes his glance intently upward, as he grasps in both hands his great two-handed sword. The design is curiously suggestive of the religious feeling influencing the knights and cavaliers of the middle ages. The contrast between the still, mystical light of the chapel and the rigid but powerful human form, is very striking; while there is interest, technically speaking, in the effect of early day-

No. 410. *"Site of an Early Christian Altar."*
John Pettie, R. A.

"The method adopted in fixing the orientation of churches by a
rod placed in the ground; the sun's rays appearing above the horizon
fixed the line of orientation."

51 × 84

light as opposed to the mechanical light of an expiring lamp
hanging between the pillars.

This picture has been purchased by the Royal Academy
out of the funds of the "Chantrey Bequest." Sir Francis Chantrey, the well-known English
sculptor, who died in 1841 without issue, left the residue of
his personal estate, amounting
to about a hundred thousand
pounds sterling, to his wife for
life, and on her decease—which
took place a few years ago—to
the Royal Academy of Arts, to
be expended in the purchase of pictures painted in England by living artists.

No. 410, *"Site of an Early Christian Altar,"* is also by Mr. Pettie. The scene illus-

47 × 65

No. 258. *"The Morning of the Battle of Agincourt."* Sir John Gilbert, R. A.

trates the method adopted for fixing the orientation of churches. A large group of priests and others is assembled in the outskirts of a forest among the trees and felled timber, watching earnestly for the first rays of the rising sun, in order to determine the site of an altar. Shading their eyes with their hands, they are just encountering the first brilliant gleams of the god of day. Apart from the dignity of thought in the subject itself, the effect of early sunlight is very skillfully rendered.

Sir John Gilbert, R. A., has chosen for the subject of his one Academy picture, "*The Morning of the Battle of Agincourt*," and has sketched for us here the three tired horsemen, which occupy nearly the whole of his picture in the large room. On the actual canvas we can see in the distance a line of warriors—the remnant of the English host—sitting, as Shakespeare describes, "like fixed candlesticks with torch-staves in their hands," and "their poor jades bob down their heads, dropping the hides and hips," and "their executors, the knavish crows, fly o'er them, all impatient for their hour." This is a valuable historical work, painted with great realism and *verve;* Sir John Gilbert having exceptional knowledge of costume and details of the period. The picture is grand in style, and full of the spirit of the scene, as given in Shakespeare's play of "King Henry V"; in fact, the artist has evidently been much more influenced by the spirit of the play than by Hume or any other historian. Sir John Gilbert is a painter in water-colors as well as in oils, and is president of the principal water-color society of England.

Next in order we may refer to some prominent associates of the Royal Academy, artists from whom the full members are elected as vacancies occur.

The only exhibited works this year by Mr. G. H. Boughton, A. R. A., are from scenes in North Holland. In Mr. Boughton's studio we see from time to time other subjects, but the English public will know this artist best in 1884 by his sturdy field-handmaidens of Brabant, and his views of that strange sea-shore in Holland, where the villagers nestle under sand-hills, protected from wind and wave by an impenetrable wall, which hides even the village church-tower from those who approach it from the sea. It is a wild and windy place at the best of times, inhabited by sturdy peasants who cultivate the flat country and make scanty harvests, both from sea and land; but it has special attractions for the artist in summer-time for the quaintness of the scene. The soft, atmospheric effects, the costumes and buildings, lend themselves readily to the artist's pencil. Mr. Boughton has told us of these things in the pages of "Harper's Magazine," and we now know something more of the color and character of North Holland by his exhibited works. Mr. Boughton's own sketch of his single-figure picture, a girl carrying a basket of cabbages, exhibits a stalwart figure worthy to be carved in stone and placed beside Mr. Hamo Thornycroft's statue of "*The Mower.*" There would be singular appropriateness in the juxtaposition of these two

3

figures, emblematic of field-labor (see "Sculpture"). On the technical quality of Mr. Boughton's art we need not dwell now; there is the usual feeling for refinement of colors in the
picture of "*The Field Handmaiden*"; the purple of the cabbages, and the brown and gray

No. 80.   "*A Field Handmaiden, Brabant.*"   G. H. BOUGHTON, A. R. A.

of the distant village, form a pleasant harmony with the fair hair and work-a-day attire of
the girl. But some day, not far distant, we hope to see Mr. Boughton in a new field of
labor altogether.

Mr. P. R. Morris, A. R. A., has the art of attracting us by his treatment of the simplest
incidents. A little child, waiting ready dressed for a drive in the park (the artist's own

child, by-the-way), was put on canvas with so much style and attractiveness that the editor of the London "Graphic" newspaper decided to reproduce it as a colored illustration in the Christmas number of that paper. The popularity thus attained by the painter, through the medium of the printing-press, is enormous, no less than six hundred and fifty thousand copies having been printed and distributed over the English-speaking world. Mr. P. R. Morris's picture may not be high art, but it is innocently attractive, and there is an air of refinement which has proved delightful to the inmates of many homes. But, as a critic justly remarks, Mr. Morris is not at his best in painting pictures of "overdressed babies, whose

No. 458. *"A Village below the Sand-Dunes"* (*"Un Village près des Dunes"*). G. H. BOUGHTON, A. R. A.

raiment is from Bond Street, and the texture of whose countenances is that of the costliest dolls in the Burlington Arcade." There is better and healthier work in his large picture of *"Sweethearts and Wives,"* which we have chosen for illustration. There is a little of the tendency to overcolor his pictures evident in this, but the old West-Indiaman, with her white-painted, yellow-stained, and weather-beaten timbers, coming into port under a summer sun, forming a background to the gay dresses of the girls on the quay, forms altogether so bright and pleasant a scene that we may thank the painter, rather than blame him, for putting so much light, air, and gayety of color into a common scene at an English seaport.

43 × 38½

No. 177. *"Quite ready."*
P. R. Morris, A. R. A.

Mr. Morris is a painter of much vivacity and originality, and everything he touches has a marked per-
sonality. Few painters are more rapid, or have greater
facility with the brush.

Of the many delicate and refined painters of *genre*
in England (men whose work is not much seen in
public exhibitions, because they paint for private com-
missions), Mr. Marcus Stone, A. R. A., is one of the
most attractive. His pictures are generally painted on
a small scale, and elaborated with the utmost care
and fastidiousness. No better example of Mr. Marcus
Stone's style could have been selected than the two
pictures, *"Fallen out"* and *"Reconciled,"* which he has
sketched for this work. The harmonious color and
careful touch of the brush must be left to the imagination. All Mr. Stone's work is thorough, and the
story of the picture is generally suggested rather than
explained. The artist is the son of Frank Stone,
R. A., the painter of *"The Last Appeal,"* and other subjects which charmed the last generation of Academy visitors. It is said that Mr. Ruskin, standing one day in front of a very
popular picture by Frank Stone, turned to the artist, who happened to be present, and said,
"Thank you, Frank." These words subsequently formed the criticism of the picture in Mr.
Ruskin's printed notes of the Academy Exhibition.

Mr. Marcus Stone, an artist from childhood and by *tradition de famille,* so to speak,
will probably soon be in the ranks
of the Royal Academy, of which he
is now an associate.

No. 798. *"Daniel in the Lions'
Den,"* by Robert Thorburn, A. R. A.
Mr. Thorburn, in whose art may
still be traced the influence of his
early training as a miniature-painter,
treats this subject in a somewhat
original manner. The prophet, an
aged, bearded man, clad in a mantle, stands in the midst of the terri-

48 × 78

No. 403. *"Sweethearts and Wives."* P. R. Morris, A. R. A.

ble beasts, among whom he has been cast by order of the king. Before him is a radiant female form—the angelic being sent by the Almighty to protect his servant. The motive of this design is, in reality, the figure of the angel, that of Daniel being comparatively of

No. 448. *"Fallen out."*   No. 449. *"Reconciled."*

MARCUS STONE, A. R. A.

"We fell out, my wife and I,
Oh, we fell out, I know not why,
And kissed again with tears."

secondary importance in the background. It was otherwise in the very remarkable picture of this subject, painted by Mr. Briton Riviere, R. A., some few years ago, and with which we are all so familiar from the engravings, wherein the whole interest of the design is made to center with surprising power in the solitary figure, with back turned to the spectator, of the grand old prophet.

No. 35. *"The Sky Lover,"* by G. A. Storey, A. R. A., is a work instinct with the quiet humor with which the artist evidently desired to invest the design. A young couple, lady and gentleman, seated on a garden-bench, are apparently afflicted with that bar to all human progress—a distressing degree of bashfulness. The lady is seated at one end of the bench, a book, upon her lap, and with eyes modestly cast down and face turned away, while she somehow advances one hand in the direction of some flowers which her admirer has ven-

No. 798.　"*Daniel in the Lions' Den.*"
ROBERT THORBURN, A.R.A.

"Then Daniel said unto the King, 'My God hath sent his angel, and hath shut the lions' mouths.'"

tured to push toward her upon the seat. He, at the other end of the bench, and holding his cap up so as to partially screen his face, looks the prey of a *mauvaise honte* which we much question if his companion altogether approves. If the poor fellow would but take heart of grace and remember that "faint heart never won fair lady," he might possibly have a better prospect of succeeding in his suit.

The Old World picturesqueness which attracted Samuel Prout and the English painters of the beginning of the century, still attracts and repays the artist. The local costumes not quite extinct, the old towers and churches, the high-pitched roofs and gables covered with carved wood-work, send many artists to Rouen and other parts of Normandy. Mr. W. J. Hennessy, living much near Honfleur, at the mouth of the Seine (whose work was in the Grosvenor Gallery), and his friend Mark Fisher, still send us pictures of Normandy orchards and bits of pastoral life. (See sketches in Grosvenor Gallery.)

Mr. Eyre Crowe, in the sketches before us, depicts more of the life and activity of the town. Rouen is a great commercial center in the north of France, and, like Birmingham in England, a "fish-center" for distribution over the country. The scene in the fish-market is seldom visited by artists, but it is worth fishing out. The old court-yard of the school at the Aître, St. Maclou, is well

No. 35.　"*The Shy Lover.*"
G. A. STOREY, A.R.A.

known, and permission can easily be obtained to sketch the wood-carving and architecture of the fifteenth century, which still exists in the cloisters and precincts of the famous church

No. 1627. *"Fish-Market at Rouen."* Eyre Crowe, A. R. A.

of St. Maclou, at Rouen. Mr. Eyre Crowe has grouped the scholars with singular dexterity in the sketch before us, and has given an interest to the scene which many an artist would have missed. It is worth while for the reader to look along the line of the young people in this illustration; there is nothing more life-like in the book.

No. 169. *"School at the Aitre, St. Maclou, Rouen."* Eyre Crowe, A. R. A.

No. 552, *The Scramble at the Wedding*, by J. B. Burgess, A. R. A., is a subject illustrating domestic life in Spain. The wedding-party is leaving the church after the ceremony, and the happy bridegroom, with his lovely wife leaning trustfully upon his arm, is acknowledging the congratulations and good wishes of many friends. The dark-eyed bride, who is glancing downward, is the cynosure of all eyes, and, in her pink dress and the ever-becoming mantilla, is a splendid realization of Spanish beauty. In the group of girls upon her right one at least looks as if she thought that she herself at one time might have had some hope of occupying the young wife's happy position. Upon the left a cavalier on horseback liberally showers small coins among the urchins and others assembled. One little lass offers a bouquet to the bride, and in the foreground *gamins* scramble furiously for the

471 × 715.

No. 552. *"The Scramble at the Wedding."* J. B. Burgess, A. R. A.

coins so liberally bestowed, and there is a pretty touch of sentiment in the incident of the little beggar-girl with her tambourine on the right, eagerly followed by the hesitating steps of her poor, old, blind grandfather. Mr. Burgess, who executed the picture, is now the most able exponent of Spanish domestic *genre* subjects in England. Educated in the schools of the English Royal Academy, where he was a student in 1848, and a silver medalist, he was early impressed with a great admiration of the works of the late John Phillip, R. A., whose manner of art he has adopted—without, however, the least degree of servile imitation. Mr. Burgess has spent a considerable time in Spain, where he has accumulated a vast number of sketches done upon the spot as material for future pictures. Unlike Mr. Edwin Long, R. A., and other followers of the school of John Phillip, who have forsaken Spanish subjects for other branches of art, Mr. Burgess has found in Spain, its

FAITH.
E. ARMITAGE, R. A.

customs, people, and climate, a motive for art-work of which he has never been weary, and from his first more important picture "*Brave Toro*," to the present time, he has followed with unfailing fidelity the delineation of Spanish life and character. The artist exhibits two other pictures at the Academy in portraits of E. A. Goodall, Esq., and the Honorable Mrs. H. A. Laurence, but, clever though they undoubtedly are, we have no desire to see the artist abandon for portraiture what is beyond all question his real *rôle* in art.

Mr. Luke Fildes, A. R. A., has sketched the central figure of his chief contribution to the Academy entitled "*Venetian Life*," No. 390. This artist is one whose genius will not

No. 390. "*Venetian Life.*" LUKE FILDES, A. R. A.

be denied. It was but a few years ago that he startled the world of art with his picture of "*Casuals*"—a work so powerful, instructive, and impressive that, had he but followed on with other productions of like quality, his future fame was assured. In succeeding years we had from his brush "*The Widower*," and other subjects, strong in individuality, but with a uniform character of melancholy in motive than was hardly to be desired. Determined to free himself from the reputation of being painter of dismal subjects only, the young artist has this year struck out a totally new line for himself, and that, it is only fair to add, with complete success. Mr. Fildes has been to Venice, where his brother-in-law, Henry Woods,

4

A. R. A. resides; and, in that city of marble palaces and generally bright influences, the inspiration he desired came to him. He painted on the spot a large picture illustrating everyday "Venetian life." In the Piazza del Marco, or in the grand places of that peerless city one does not see the real life of Venice, but let the visitor, in the evening, traverse some of the by-ways and he will notice groups of work-girls and others, who, seated at the entrances of the palaces, in which even the poorest now lodge, ply needle and thread, have their long dark hair combed out, and meantime make the air vocal with songs and chatter. Dressed in costumes the lightest and sometimes the most brilliant in color, and with busy fingers and not less active tongues, very often these characteristic groups pass the best part of the night thus engaged, under the lovely blue sky of the famous southern city. A wonderfully pretty girl, with rich, reddish-colored hair, is seated, holding a ball of thread and some muslin on her lap. She is dressed in light blue, and her costume, like that of her companions, is bright and pretty in the extreme. Mr. Fildes is to be congratulated upon changing

No. 1546. *"Pressing to the West."* HUBERT HERKOMER, A. R. A.

his class of subject in his pictures. We admit the strength, expression, and value of his former designs, but there was always the fear that he might have fallen away, as an illustrator of only one class of subjects, and that a morbid one. Another picture by this artist is a Venetian flower-girl, a figure nearly life-size, with blue-black, curly hair, in bright-green shawl and gay dress, standing near a blaze of flowers. Thus, the Venice of to-day, described so well by Mr. W. D. Howells, and painted with such subtilty and grace by Van Haanen, is depicted without much reticence of color, but with unmistakable power.

No. 810. *"The Saturday Dole in Worcester Chapter-House."* VAL PRINCEP, A. R. A.

Mr. Hubert Herkomer, A. R. A., sends to the Academy the picture of *"Pressing to the West,"* the studies for which he made when visiting America last year. This artist, who thirty-three years ago himself landed at New York city from Bavaria, and was taken by his parents to Cleveland, Ohio, was much struck by the picturesque aspect of the scene in Castle Garden, in the dreary building set apart for immigrants at the present time. Here was material exactly suited to a painter of Mr. Herkomer's temperament, imagination, and energy. The accompanying sketch will indicate, to those who did not see the unfinished original in New York, how the painter has worked out his idea, bringing together the various nationalities, and grouping them in one powerful, pathetic picture. It is a drama of many acts brought before us in one scene.

It may be interesting to note how a picture, which created much interest in New York during its progress, was received in England by the press. "We have little doubt," says the

"Pall Mall Gazette," "that this gloomy and singular composition will be the most popular picture of the year." The London "Observer" says, "The execution seems purposely rough, and the color brown and unpleasant, but it is painted with prodigious vigor"; and the

6 x 6.

No. 430. "*Romeo and Juliet*." FRANK DICKSEE.

"Daily News" speaks of it as "a composition which has no mission of beauty, and is instructive rather than agreeable."

As an artistic effort this picture will scarcely add to the reputation of the painter of "*The Last Muster*." The skill is undeniable, and few painters could bring together such a variety of character with more force and individuality—the easy-going Irish, the Germans, Hungarians, Poles, Italians, and others—but the handling is decidedly rough, and the picture seems to want relief—if not a touch of actual comedy, at least that grim relief that Hogarth would have given to such a scene.

No. 810, "*The Saturday Dole in Worcester Chapter-House: A Relic of the Olden Time,*" by Val Prinsep, A.R.A. This is the interesting record of a charitable bequest to the poor of the city of Worcester. A large quantity of bread is distributed under the superintendence of the clergy in the chapter-house, and the gathering of old and young upon these occasions of those, not unfrequently, who, but for this most seasonable charity, would be in dire want, is a sight calculated to arouse feelings both of benevolence and gratitude.*

The painter of "*Romeo and Juliet,*" Mr. Frank Dicksee, whose illustrations to Longfellow's "Evangeline" are well known, made a great success in the Academy in 1877 by a picture called "*Harmony,*" a girl seated at an organ and a young man listening. It was an ambitious work for a young artist, but it was excellently placed in the center of a wall in the first gallery, purchased by the Academy, and afterward engraved. Since that time Mr. Dicksee has exhibited annually important pictures, and in 1881 was made an Associate of the Academy. There is very beautiful painting in his parting of "*Romeo and Juliet,*" with

48 × 108.

No. 805. "*A Fen Farm.*" ROBERT W. MACBETH, A.R.A.

"Cusha! cusha! cusha! calling,
For the dews will soon be falling."

the light of morning breaking in the distance and just tingeing the laurel-leaves as the lovers part. It is a powerful picture, much finer, we imagine, than the majority of visitors to the Academy discovered, as it hung in a corner of a gallery. However, an engraving is

---

* In the absence of a sketch of this picture by the artist, we have inserted a photographic reproduction by the Lehmann process. It will serve to indicate the composition.

in progress which will give the details of costume and texture as they have never yet been seen. There is no doubt that the painting of details and the effect of break of day are the artist's strong points in this work. But the painter of "Evangeline," in 1879, with the emigrants on the shore, "when the sun went down," has a reserve of power of which we shall hear more in future exhibitions.

No. 805, "*A Fen Farm*," by Robert Walker Macbeth, A. R. A., is one of the Cambridgeshire or Lincolnshire scenes in which the artist delights. In a farm in the low, marshy land of the fen districts, a buxom, golden-haired country lassie stands at the farm-

No. 881. "*After Culloden: Rebel-Hunting.*" Seymour Lucas.

gate she is holding open, while she lustily calls into their night's resting-place her charge of young cattle. The cows and calves obey the familiar invitation, but watch warily the dog standing close to his mistress's side. The sky is rendered luminous by the setting sun, which also brightens, with its departing radiance, the living objects in the scene. Mr. Macbeth, who is a Scotch artist, was born in Glasgow in 1848, and may be considered fortunate in being elected an Associate of the Academy while still so young. He has not followed the line of art of his father, Norman Macbeth, the well-known portrait-painter, but there can be little doubt that the early artistic associations and training which fell to his lot have been of no little value in securing his hitherto remarkably successful career.

No. 881, *"After Culloden; Rebel-Hunting,"* by Seymour Lucas, is another of the pictures purchased by the Royal Academy from the Chantrey Bequest Fund. In a Scotch smithy in the Highlands, after the Duke of Cumberland had, in 1746, defeated Prince Charles, the last of the Stuarts, at Culloden, some English soldiers are busy on the trail of rebel Scots. The smiths—fine, brawny fellows—are busy at their trade when the duke's soldiers, sword in hand, enter. Whether these good fellows—or any of them—were concerned in the recent fierce fight, which cost them between two and three thousand men slain upon the field, we will not undertake to say, but certainly more than one of their number present an appearance of determination and strength that would augur no good thing for those who are to make them prisoners and lead them off to punishment. The picture is a remarkable example of the steadily increasing powers of the young artist, Mr. Seymour Lucas. There is a little conventionality apparent in the arrangement, but the painting is thorough and the color good; and the general verdict in London is that it is "the most satisfactory purchase of the year out of the funds of the Chantrey Bequest."

No. 559, *"Consulting the Oracle,"* by J. W. Waterhouse. Last year this artist exhibited at the Academy a picture of the Emperor Honorius—a scene in Italian court-life in the fifth or sixth century. This picture excited attention as a work of considerable promise, but it scarcely led the way to so fine a production technically as the one we have now to

48 × 78.

No. 559. "Consulting the Oracle." J. W. Waterhouse.

remark upon. The subject Mr. Waterhouse has selected is singular, as it relates to a practice among the Eastern nations in ancient times, when they slaughtered a man, cut off his head, and put it in spices and oil. They then wrote the name of an evil spirit on a golden plate, placed it under the tongue, and, the head being fastened to the wall and lamps lighted,

they knelt down in adoration, when it was said the tongue began to utter divinations.
Such was the singular idea of this particular oracle, the diviners becoming so excited that
they imagined they heard a voice whispering future events. The artist's design shows to us
the interior of a temple with marble floor, and upon the left is affixed to the wall the
ghastly human head, in front of which the diviner is listening to the imaginary words of
terrible import, and repeating them to a group of women, seated around in a semicircle.

34 × 26.

No. 14. *"The Very Image."* JOSEPH CLARK.

The character in the listeners is remarkable. Some are bowed down with anguish at the
message just conveyed to them; others are hopeful; and others, again, are listening in rapt
attention. The costumes are varied and beautiful, the expressions of the faces also being
well expressed. The semi-obscurity of the building, lighted by oil-lamps burning before the
face of the dead, the natural excitement of the diviner, and the semicircle of listeners in
the spring-time of life, form altogether a remarkable picture—remarkable especially for good
color and quality.

No. 14, "*The Very Image*," by Joseph Clark. The group here consists of a young artist standing, palette and brushes in hand, in some humble country cottage. He has just finished his picture standing upon the easel, which an old granddame is expressing high approval of, while her good man indorses her opinion, and their little chubby grandson sits upon the floor doing all the mischief, time will admit of, with the artist's camp-stool. The picture on the easel may be the interior of the cottage itself, with the admiring old couple introduced, and perhaps the child; but, at any rate, the picture is admired, and the painter has the satisfaction of having an approving critic. The contrast of stalwart manhood with trembling old age, and the charm of childhood, will also not be overlooked by the observant. For many years (without any special recognition from the

No. 15. "*Idle Moments*,"
C. E. PERUGINI.

Academy) has Mr. Joseph Clark had similar subjects on the walls, interiors painted with the precision and certainty of the old Dutch masters; and, like them, making every detail of household life an interesting part of the composition.

A refined and graceful picture, gray in tone, lighted by a touch of blue in the peacock's plume, is Mr. Perugini's "*Idle Moments*." The action of drawing the feathers through the hand gives the motive of the composition. This artist's method of painting is highly finished and careful, resembling in its style that of Sir Frederick Leighton. Mr. Perugini married Kate, daughter of the late Charles Dickens. This lady's portraits of children are very successful, and are generally seen in our exhibition.

No. 880. "*A Venetian Girl going to the Well*."
HILDA MONTALBA.

A young member of the talented family of the Montalbas is represented (No. 880) in a Venetian girl going to a well; her sister Ellen is a most skillful portrait-painter, and exhibited two portraits of ladies this year. Examples of the work of Clara and H. S. Montalba will be found in this volume.

Among the younger painters whose work is of great interest and promise we should mention Mr. Herbert Schmalz. No picture this year excited more interest during its progress than "*Too late*," a large and carefully thought-our picture, exhibiting great power on the part of the painter. The solemn grouping of the figures round the body of the bride, the management of color in the morning light, and the painting of the interior and accessories of the palace of a Norse chieftain on a very large canvas, went far to make a great success. But the figure of the returning warrior, who arrives to find his young wife dead, is less successful than the rest of the picture. Mr. Schmalz had another picture in the Grosvenor Gallery.

No. **827.** *"Too late!"* Herbert Schmalz.

Of Mr. J. D. Linton, of whose fine picture of *"The Declaration of War"* we give a reproduction, we have spoken in the section devoted to water-colors. It will be interesting, however, to give a sketch of his principal works in oils, communicated by the artist, which appeared in a London newspaper:

"The President of the Royal Institute of Painters in Water-Colors has made a reputation as an oil-painter principally by a single series of pictures. This is the only way in which we can account for the fact that one of the first craftsmen of the age remains outside the ranks of the Royal Academy. That body considers painting in oils as alone worthy of its attention, and, until 1880, Mr. Linton was simply one of the best of living water-color painters. But in 1879 he had the happy inspiration of furnishing a great room with five large oil-pictures, representing the life of a soldier in the sixteenth century. It will not be the least notable fact about the Royal Academy of 1884 that it will contain the best installment of this extremely interesting series. The five pictures have not been exhibited in their proper order. This is their true distribution: '*The Declaration of War*,' Royal Academy, 1884; '*The Benediction*,' Royal Academy, 1881; '*The Surrender*,' Royal Academy, 1883; '*Victorious*,' Grosvenor Gallery, 1880; '*The Banquet*,' Royal Academy,

THE PET PLANT.
H. S. MARKS, R.A.

1882. The legend running through them may be thus rapidly defined: A young soldier is in the service of a German prince who declares war against the Turk; he is solemnly blessed and knighted in the cathedral; he attacks the principal fortress of the Turk and storms it; he returns to his prince covered with glory; and is honored with a public banquet of congratulation. It may be a matter of some interest to mention that throughout the series many of the heads are portraits. The young prince is Mr. E. J. Gregory, A. R. A.; his minister of state is Mr. Brewtnall, the distinguished water-color painter, and the faces of several other kindred artists may be detected by the curious.

"The picture of this year, '*The Declaration of War*,' though the last painted, is the first of the series. We stand in the interior of a Byzantine palace, which, presumably, from the order of its architecture and the nature of its ornaments, stands not far from the Adriatic—in Istria, perhaps, or Dalmatia—although the arms which we see embroidered in gold and black on the blue arras are the arms of Bohemia. At the top of a low flight of marble steps, the young prince of the state, Herzog or Landesherr, owning no suzerain but the Kaiser, stands in a splendid attitude of wrath, rending the parchment treaty which the two stolid embassadors from the Grand Turk, who stand below him on the left-hand side, have brought. The embassadors bow with a dignified resignation, but evidently all the Germans sympathize with their prince. Behind him, from one door, the Church gives him her support in a stream of priests and acolytes, headed by a blonde Teutonic bishop. On the other side the slender young soldier, a mere stripling in armor, who is to be the hero of the series, is presented as general of the coming war by the minister of state, who advances in a long robe of *mir*. At the left-hand corner of the picture the lawyers form a picturesque group over their codes and Latin formulas. The color of the whole picture is sumptuous. The simple green and red of the flowing robes of the embassadors contrast with the elaborate richness of the prince's dress. By the Turks, on a carved marble seat of florid Renaissance work, stand the useless gifts which they have brought with them from their Orient.

"Mr. Linton thinks it yet possible that he may be tempted to add an appendix to the series. He would like to represent his soldier in old age, still wearing the costume of his glorious youth, and serving a new young Herzog, whose ways are not his, and whose fashions are half a century later."

Mr. Linton has also exhibited several small and very powerful pictures in oils, principally in the Grosvenor Gallery in 1879.

In the year 1876 a poetical picture, by Mr. Frederick Morgan, attracted much attention in the Royal Academy. It was a large work, representing hay-makers returning from work in the glow of a summer's evening. Since that time this artist has been a regular contribufor to the exhibitions, but he has seldom painted with more success than in 1884. We have noticed elsewhere his picture of children, but the present sketch (No. 147, "*Besieged*") indicates his principal work. It is accurate in the lines of the composition (for it is by the artist's own hand), but gives little idea of the skillful management of sunlight on the features of the woman and child, or of the delicate balance of color throughout. This picture, happy in idea, natural in action, presents us with a scene of rustic life in summer on the southern side of the Alps.

No. 147. "*Besieged*."   FREDERICK MORGAN.   36 × 45.

No. 701, "*La Cocarde Tricolore*," by G. P. Jacomb-Hood. A young mother standing at a window in Paris, rocking her child's cradle with one foot while she sews together the fatal tricolor cockade her husband is to wear in that awful period of French history to which the picture refers. The incident recalls memories never to be forgotten in the history not only of "*la belle France*" but of Europe. A great nation roused to wrath by a long system of cruelty and oppression that was unendurable; the consequent destruction of king, queen, and nobles, who, either willingly or by force of circumstances, had become oppressors and brought to one of the fairest and most beautiful of cities a "Reign of Terror," a very carnival of blood. Over that time we may willingly draw a veil, when the fierce passions

of man were in all their fury. But the French Revolution is ever a favorite subject with the painter. Here
is the young wife of a Paris *ouvrier* busily plying
needle and thread, constructing the distinctive badge
which by-and-by is to be worn by her husband at that
terrible festival of the guillotine. Will she also be one
of the many of her sex who used to sit, as at a theatre,
calmly working while the bloody massacres were going
on? At present she looks thoughtful and as if half
alarmed at the tumult in the streets below, and we
care not to think how she may soon be an approving
participator in the scenes of blood taking place around.
This picture is one of the successes of the year by a
young exhibitor.

No. 693, "*Disinherited*," by Laslett J. Pott. The
scene here depicted reminds us of Hogarth's "*Rake's
Progress*." It is the oft-told story of the lavish thought-
lessness and waste of youth. A young man, after doubt-

No. 1622. "*The Marsh-King's Daughter.*" JOHN SCOTT.

less countless follies, and as constant forgiveness, has at length aroused his father's wrath,
has met with the reward of his misdeeds, and is seen
descending the stairs of the mansion a beggar. There
is no mistake about it, for the scene tells its own story
most powerfully. The young man has been a spend-
thrift, squanderer, and at last comes the day of reckon-
ing when the outraged parent, who has heard the oft-
repeated tale of his son's offenses, until the time of
forgiveness is gone, stands indignantly at the head of
the stairs ordering the offender to depart from his
house. But there is still a pleading voice to be heard
in favor of young scapegrace, and, come what may, a
mother's love is not to be exhausted. And thus we
see the mother striving to allay the storm of just indignation; but all is useless, and with bowed head and
humbled mien the heir of the house quits his father's
house, while the servants, as their young master passes
from his home forever, by their respectful obeisance

No. 693. "*Disinherited.*" L. J. POTT.

suggest that possibly the young sinner was, after all, not wholly unpopular, and may have been his own greatest enemy. The artist, Mr. L. J. Pott, has more than once, in exhibited works of very considerable power, made fair bid for the honor of associateship, which, if he is but true to himself in the way in which he is now working, may hardly be much longer denied to him.

No. 374. "*The Peace-Maker*," by G. B. O'Neill (sketched on page 46), a group in which a little girl is attempting to re-establish the *entente cordiale* between two school-boys who have fallen out, is an interesting and satisfactory little study of the class to which we have been now referring.

No. 662, "*Saved from the Snow*," by Arthur Stocks. A group consisting of a shepherd and his family gathered round a small lamb which the man holds upon his knees. The

No. 662. "*Saved from the Snow*." A. STOCKS.

weather has been hard, and perhaps, far away from its mother, in some wild mountain-pass, the poor little lamb has been overcome in a snow storm, and would have perished but that the shepherd's footstep strayed that way and he saved the wanderer. And now, safely housed in the good man's cottage, with warmth, food, and kindly treatment, the pretty animal will be restored. Rather a quaint feature of the design is the shepherd's dog— certainly an animal not naturally fond of sheep, but who is now seated, looking on at what is going forward, almost with instinctive knowledge that, with good luck and nursing, the time may come when he will have the pleasure of harrying and driving this little nursling with the rest of the flock. There is great pictorial interest in Mr. Stocks's pictures, which are looked for annually as popular points in the exhibition. We believe "*Saved from the Snow*" will shortly appear as an engraving.

No. 516. "*The French in Cairo,* A. D. 1800." WALTER C. HORSLEY.

Mr. Walter C. Horsley, son of the well-known Royal Academician, J. C. Horsley, has turned to good account his experiences as an artist, or war correspondent, on one of the London illustrated newspapers, and, nearly every year, since 1877 (when he first made a mark with a picture called "*The Hour of Prayer,*" a scene on a Turkish ironclad), he has contributed some painting descriptive of life in the East and the incidents of modern warfare. The value of this early training in the sketching and arrangement of groups of figures is conspicuous in this artist's work, which is generally well placed on the line in the Royal Academy. This year he has chosen an historical incident in which he depicts a successful soldier of the Emperor Napoleon cutting in the stone of one of the principal buildings in

Cairo the names of the great marshals of France. Some of these names still remain, a memorial of the emperor's love of display, and of his merciless disregard of the feelings of those he conquered. In the group Mr. Horsley pictures, the French soldiers contemplate with satisfaction the work of their comrade, who, with chisel and mallet, carves out the famous names, while the citizens look on with feelings of bitterness and indignation at the insult thus put upon them and their noble city. One French soldier, a veteran from many a hard-fought field, is sitting down reading in a newspaper the account of some recent battle, while a young comrade, with musket slung at his back, is also seated, observing, with nonchalant ease and an expression of gratified pride, the public record of his country's prowess.

No. 128, "*The Union-Jack*," by W. Christian Symons, is one of those strongly designed, bright, and suggestive subjects that is sure to be deservedly popular. Some girls and others are wandering near a flag-staff on the sea-shore, when a Jack-tar amuses himself by wrapping the flag of Old England round a bright-faced, happy-looking lass. And many a time before has the Union-Jack sheltered and protected those in our little island, as Nelson

No. **128.**   "*The Union-Jack*."   W. C. SYMONS.

and many other heroes could have testified. The other lassies and surrounding spectators look on amused at the impromptu garment honest Jack has found for his lass, but little cares he, while his strong, sheltering arm is placed around the fair form, trusting confidingly in him.

No. 294, "*Men were Deceivers ever,*" by Peter Macnab. The artist here hints, it is to be surmised, at one of those stories of fond but fleeting love, which ever have been since the world began. A young gentleman is speaking his devotion to his sweetheart as he tenderly presses her hand, and at the same time we see in the distance the ship which is

36 × 28.

No. 294. "*Men were Deceivers ever.*" PETER MACNAB.

" Sigh no more, ladies, sigh no more,
Men were deceivers ever;
One foot on sea, and one on shore,
To one thing constant never."

to bear him to other shores, and perhaps to other loves. The maiden looks very trustful and equally sad, so that one quite feels for her in her bereavement. Perhaps it is unwise to trust a lover—particularly if he be young and handsome—miles away in a ship, if he must be gone a long time. There is a sad and tender grace about the treatment

No. 828. *"An Impromptu."* H. T. Schäfer.

of the well-worn theme peculiar to Mr. Macnab's work. The picture will make a good engraving.

Next are two representative pictures by H. T. Schäfer, a young and successful painter, a frequent contributor to the Academy. No. 828, *"An Impromptu,"* is a pretty idyl; two Greek girls, fair and graceful, listening to a classic shepherd who pipes sweet music while they listen, charmed by the melody.

No. 419, *"Il Dolce far Niente,"* from the same brush, pictures another fair dame stretched at her ease among clustering flowers, in the distance being what are possibly the blue waters of the Grecian Archipelago. The lady has one arm raised above her head, and looks the very personification of all that is graceful and lovely. Mr. Schäfer is sometimes over-bright in color, but his grace of line bears down all criticism; no one is a harder worker in this branch of art. It is worth while to note here how admirably the artist has indicated the flow of soft drapery in his sketch (419) before us. Few artists have greater facility of expression in line.

No. 419. *"Il Dolce far Niente."* H. T. Schäfer.

No. 425. "*The Widower*," by William Rainey, is a study of an old cottager, left by fortune to fight the battle of life alone, when he is of an age ill fitting him for the contest. The poor old fellow is cleaning his cup after partaking of that beverage without which it

No. 425. "*The Widower.*" WILLIAM RAINEY.

would almost appear that the poor in England could hardly exist. He looks desperately lonely, and we need not be told of the irremediable loss he has experienced. This picture is by a young artist who made a mark last year by an excellent river-scene entitled "*The Horse-Boat, Fowey.*"

The works of Mr. Wetherbee and Mr. Waterlow may be examined together. They are

No. 414. *"The Harvest is past, the Summer is ended."* G. F. WETHERBEE.

painters of kindred subjects, both in oils and water-colors. Mr. E. A. Waterlow is a young and very successful painter of landscape with figures, showing, like Mr. Wetherbee, much

No. 916. *"Sand-Digging, North Cornwall."* ERNEST A. WATERLOW.

of the feeling of the late Frederick Walker in pastoral subjects. But Mr. Waterlow is no imitator of other men's styles; he is working out steadily a line of his own, with a good eye for color and grace in composition. This year his picture of "*Sand-Digging in North Cornwall*" reminds us in its treatment more of Mr. J. C. Hook, R.A.

No. 809. "*La Belle Dame sans Merci.*" ANNA LEA MERRITT.

> "She took me to her elfin grot,
>   And there she wept, and sighed full sore,
> And there I shut her wild, wild eyes
>   With kisses four.
> And there she lulled me asleep,
>   And there I dreamed—ah! woe betide
> The latest dream I ever dreamed
>   On the cold hill's side."

   Mrs. Merritt's large canvas, "*La Belle Dame sans Merci,*" occupies a very prominent position in the center of the wall in Gallery VII. The picture is full of grace; there is fine drawing of the figure, as usual. The accessories have been painted with great care; the elfin grot, the trees, and undergrowth, from nature-studies, giving great interest to the composition. The subject of this picture is suggested by Keats's poem of "*La Belle Dame sans Merci*"; the moment chosen is when the knight is being lulled to sleep.

No. 374. *"The Peace-Maker."* G. B. O'Neill.

No. 176. *"Old Friends."* Carl Schloesser.

"A Load of Turf." A. O'Kelly.

No. 451. *"Prince Rupert."* Stanley Berkley.

No. 815. *"Her own Gleanings."* H. R. Robertson.

SWEETHEARTS AND WIVES.
P. R. Morris, A. R. A.

No. 674, "*Called to Court*," by Haynes Williams. "She thought of nothing but the bright life before her, and in her youth and innocence dreamed only of love and truth and pleasure; but he, her father, sighed and wished that France's queen had left his child to him and home." Mr. Williams, whose direct *rôle* in art one has been accustomed to regard as more akin to that of his old friend and comrade, Mr. J. B. Burgess, A. R. A., in the present work forsakes Spanish subjects, in which, on former occasions, he has shown that he delights and has great facility, and favors us with an example of his skill in historical *genre.* The scene is laid in the time of Louis XIII, whose queen was in the habit of selecting her maids of honor on account both of their beauty and high birth. In the present instance the choice has fallen upon a very lovely girl, who, sumptuously attired in white

36 x 60.

No. 674. "*Called to Court*." HAYNES WILLIAMS.

satin, is being conducted by the old nobleman, her father, to the presence-chamber of the queen. She, in the joyousness of her young life, thinks only of the honor conferred upon her, and of coming pleasures; but her father, with greater knowledge of court-life, has other and graver thoughts. Meantime, the fair young beauty leans lightly upon her father's arm, and is more intent upon the attendant arranging her train than aught more important. Two pages, in blue-satin jackets, make obeisance as they hold open the folding-doors which lead to the immediate presence of royalty.

To turn to something designed and executed in a more comic vein. No. 671, "*Not worth Powder and Shot*," by J. C. Dollman, is certainly humorous. A mounted highwayman, armed, masked, and doubtless keenly anxious for his prey, has spied a traveler in the distance, and, setting spurs to his horse, he after a long and sharp gallop has succeeded in coming up with the individual. But, pulling up, for his horse is blown, he finds that this

No. 671. *"Not worth Powder and Shot."* J. C. DOLLMAN.

time, at any rate, he is thoroughly mistaken, for what he doubtless hoped was a wealthy traveler proved to be but a starveling, old, itinerant musician—one whose poverty is such that, feeling secure in his total lack of this world's goods, he does not even take the trouble to turn upon his heel to see who his pursuer may be, but trudges along, supremely independent in that he has nothing to lose. The subject is no caricature, no exaggeration of very unlikely possibilities, but the incident is a simple transcript of what might very well take place, while it is, of course, a humorous phase of human nature.

No. 69. *"Fact and Fiction."* G. W. C. HUTCHINSON.

No. 661, "*The Unconverted Cavalier*," by Charles C. Seton, is another work in which the motive is distinctly jocular. One of King Charles's worldling and unregenerate Cavaliers, richly attired and lounging at his ease in a chair, smoking, is listening to a Puritan who, with eager zeal, is expounding the word to him. But the good seed is evidently sown on barren soil, for the reprobate listens, too lazy even to answer, too careless to attempt to refute the words of the worthy Roundhead.

To refer to yet one other study of the class we are alluding to. No. 69, "*Fact and Fiction*," by George W. C. Hutchinson, is a quaintly characteristic figure of a little girl kneeling at a stove toasting some bread, while eyes and mind are engaged with a story-book spread open at her feet. The milk boils over on the stove, and the steam from the kettle threatens a similar mishap, the toast burns

No. 485. "*For Sale*."
ARTHUR HACKER.

furiously, but the little one's mind is in the region of fancy, and all things sublunary are lost to her. This charming little study, which exhibits the grace of childhood, is not without thoughtful sense of humor in its suggestiveness.

No. 485, "*For Sale*," by Arthur Hacker, exhibits an Arab salesman with a matchlock and various other wares which he is offering for sale. At his side runs a little black lad, and in the foreground are fruits and other objects upon a stall.

No. 439. "*Home, Sweet Home*."
W. E. F. BRITTEN.

No. 439. "*Home, Sweet Home*," by William E. F. Britten. Two country children, a boy and girl, are finding their way home through the heavy winter snows, and, as they approach, hail those who are welcoming them at the cottage-door.

No. 465. "*The Gladiator's Wife*," by E. Blair Leighton. This picture, notwithstanding the scant courtesy with which it was treated by the hangers, was one of the most interesting and remarkable in the exhibition. It recalls to mind imperial Rome when, in the splendor of her power, she inaugurated those deadly sports with wild beasts, and combats, which delighted the citizens with scenes of blood. Founded in cruelty —for it was built by Vespasian with the enforced labor of the miserable, conquered Jews—the Coliseum during the reigns of

No. 465. "*The Gladiator's Wife.*"

E. BLAIR LEIGHTON.

several succeeding emperors was the scene where the people congregated to witness the gladiatorial encounters — fights with wild beasts — and upon one occasion, at least, the wholesale destruction of the then despised sect of Christians, that served to make holiday for a warlike but semi-barbarous nation. But while demoralized by the cultivation of their more cruel instincts, and degraded by their constant trade of war, it may not be doubted that they were still susceptible to the feelings of natural affection which make "the whole world kin." It is true that even women used upon occasions to figure in their gladiatorial shows as combatants, but it is probable that such instances were comparatively isolated and unusual. Mr. Blair Leighton, in his singularly dramatic and powerful picture, depicts what would be a very probable incident, the young wife of a gladiator awaiting the result of a combat in which her husband is engaged. The splendid and terrible scene is sufficiently indicated — the immense amphitheatre crowded with spectators; the emperor in all his semi-barbaric pomp; the vestal virgins, senators, patricians, and citizens of all classes, watching with eager interest the incidents of the bloody fray. But here, unable to turn her face toward the awful sight — to the scene which may rob her, in a moment, of one dear to her as life — a young wife stands listening to the shouts and cries which greet her ear. In nervous dread she clutches at her necklace. What cares she for emperor and court, for the splendor of the scene, or for victory, if but the one life she holds so dear be spared? And meantime the brilliant light of the sun, scarce checked by the awning, is shed upon the scene as if in mockery at human happiness or woes. The artist's pathetic little story is told with wondrous power and effect.

Another work by the same hand, No. 1552, "*Conquest*," pictures an armed knight returning to his castle with what it is to be presumed are the spoils of war. Advancing with measured step and holding his trusty sword, he is preceding a lady who, with eyes cast down and humbled mien, follows her captor. An attendant is gathering up

No. 1552. "*Conquest.*"

E. BLAIR LEIGHTON.

some golden cups and other spoil at the knight's side, and in the distance others are approaching bearing in the wounded. There is perhaps a little obscurity in the design as far as the lady-prisoner is concerned, as one hardly supposes that in ages of chivalry noble knights warred against women. But certain it is that in all times and ages warriors have been keenly alive to the commercial part of their business, so it is perhaps the case that the fair dame represents a good ransom.

No. 475. "*Shadows,*" by Robert Hillingford, Oliver Cromwell seated in a chair moodily regarding a whole-length portrait of Charles I. At the Protector's side stands a lady, possibly his favorite daughter, Mrs. Claypole, and in the background is a gentleman having the appearance of being a follower of the royal cause. It is not difficult to imagine what

No. 475. "*Shadows.*"   ROBERT HILLINGFORD.

may be the feelings of mingled doubt, hesitation, and regret in the mind of the remarkable man who, in 1649, had altered a nation's destiny and signed the death-warrant of a king. Cromwell was no believer in "the divine right" of kings, but he was a patriot and a man of unflinching will. When the wrong-headed, overbearing, and obstinate monarch, unhappy Charles I, had, by his unjust acts, pressed his subjects to the verge of revolution, the people's cause found support, and themselves a most powerful leader, in the young country gentleman who was in the future to rule the kingdom. But the struggle must have been a fierce one, and particularly in the then state of public feeling, before Cromwell could have made up his mind to get rid of the king by ordering his execution. Branded on the one hand as a regicide, and on the other regarded as the saviour of his country, he must indeed have felt it to be a stern necessity, and one that taxed to the utmost even his iron will, before he could sign that fatal warrant which sent his king to the block. Naturally reticent and a man of few words, Cromwell was one to act rather than to speak, but still the shadow of that tremendous deed must have overspread his life, and it is in one of the gloomy moments of doubt and retrospection that Mr. Hillingford supposes him to be in his picture.

No. 260. *"Sporting with the Leaves that fall."* EDGAR BARCLAY.

In some sort in association with this work, No. 451, *"Prince Rupert,"* by Stanley Berkley (see sketch on page 46), represents a cavalry charge, headed by the brave, impetuous, but thoughtless prince, who perhaps helped more to mar than make the fortunes of his royal master, Charles I. The scene here pictured is most likely incidental in character

No. 356. *"The Champion of the Tournament."* G. W. JOY.

rather than being a reference to any special occasion. It could not be the battle of either Marston Moor or Naseby, for both were fought in the summer-time, while, in this design, mad Rupert and his no less wild troopers are tearing, at headlong gallop, over snow-covered marshes. At such fiery charges no one was better than Prince Rupert, but he sadly lacked discretion, and was consequently but a very poor general officer. His career was a curiously checkered one, for, first a cavalry-officer, he was afterward a naval commander, when he was well chased over the seas by Blake, and had his ships sunk and destroyed; while, after the Restoration, he turned philosopher, artist, engraver, and student of mechanics.

No. 356, *"The Champion of the Tournament,"* by George William Joy, is the portrait of a pretty-looking girl, whose tennis-bat and the balls she holds in her hands sufficiently indicate the game of skill in which she excels.

No. 1642, "*Saying Grace*," by Laura Alma-Tadema. The gifted artist vies with her husband, although in a totally different direction, in talent. Mr. Alma-Tadema, as we are aware, has a strong archæological and antiquarian taste in art, and in that particular line he is, perhaps, unequaled in the present day. A somewhat characteristic story of Mr. Tadema has found currency with reference to the prefix, *Alma*, before what was really his proper name, *Tadema*. With that ready forethought which is peculiar to him, he is said to have observed that Tadema came among the T's, and was therefore nearly last in the alphabet, while a prefix with A, as an initial letter, would make his name stand among the first in the Royal Academy catalogue and elsewhere—hence the name Alma, which he henceforth adopted. His wife, Mrs.

No. 1642. "*Saying Grace.*"
Mrs. Alma-Tadema.

Alma-Tadema, whose picture, "*Saying Grace*," we are referring to, has hitherto made as her subjects for illustration domestic incidents, and those scenes of every-day life which are not without dramatic interest and pathos. Mrs. Tadema is fond of Dutch character and costume, and that from associations which it is easy to understand. In her picture in the Academy, the family (three children with the mother and grandmother) is assembled at dinner, and a lesson of reverent thankfulness is taught in the charming group.

No. 1566. "*What shall I sing?*" (*Interior of a Cairo Café.*) F. A. Bridgman.

No. 1566, "*What shall I sing?*" Interior of a Cairo *café*, by F. A. Bridgman. This subject, which might have suited the pencil of Mr. Carl Haag, represents a couple of Egyptian gentlemen seated at their ease—one with the eternal *nargheel* in his hand—in a *café*, while a young girl, a wandering musician, asks what she shall sing to amuse them. The picture carries with it evidence of either having been painted on the spot, or from sketches made in Cairo, for character, costume, and even the sunny atmosphere of the East, are all realized with the most telling effect.

No. 46, "*A Little Outcast*," by Henriette Corkran. This artist, who is almost better known from her efforts to revive in this country the nearly extinct art of pastel-drawing,

69 × 33

No. 339. *" Herodias and her Daughter." J. R. Weguelin.*

here exhibits a rather pathetic study of one of the waifs and strays of the metropolis. A poor flower-girl, looking suppliant and piteous, holds in her hand bunches of beautiful violets for which she is eagerly seeking a purchaser.

No. 339. *"Herodias and her Daughter"* (St. Mark vi. 22-24), by J. R. Weguelin. The Scriptural incident of the foul murder of John the Baptist in prison, by command of Herod, has been a very favorite one with artists, and we have had pictured representations of the beautiful but evil-minded Salome, with the Baptist's head in a charger, innumerable. But the present rendering of the story is somewhat a new one, in that the design here shows the mother of the girl, just after her daughter had pleased the king with her dancing, whispering the foul words of vengeance into the girl's ear, which suggested, as a reward, the demand for the life

of the unhappy prophet. Every student of Scripture history is aware that John the Baptist had incurred the hatred of the king's wife, Herodias, as the prophet had lifted up his voice in condemnation of Herod's incestuous marriage. The opportunity for vengeance arrived, as Salome, on some occasion, danced before the monarch, and so pleased his sensual tastes that he swore to grant her any request she made, even to the half of his kingdom. Probably the girl, if left alone, would have demanded wealth, or something that would have gratified vanity and caprice, but, instigated by her mother, she asked for what could have given her no pleasure, the life of the man who had offended Herodias. In Mr. Weguelin's picture we see indicated in the distance the king and his court, and in the foreground the wretched girl, who lived to die a terrible death, listening to the evil words of the tempter.

Turning from biblical record to historical incident, another subject by Mr. Dicey, to whom we have previously referred, is No. 561, *"Joan of Arc in Prison."*

57 × 37

No. 561. *"Joan of Arc in Prison."* F. Dicey.

No. 124. *"Preparations for the Market, Quimperlé."*   No. 726. *"Fair Measure."* (*A Shop in Quimperlé.*)

STANHOPE A. FORBES.

in which we have the pictured semblance of the fair Maid of Orleans seated in prison, her armor by her side, and her hands grasping the hilt of her two-handed sword. The half-heroic, half-fanatic character of poor Joan is one of the most remarkable in history, and her brief life a record of some of the more unselfish and brave, as well as of the weakest, traits of our common humanity. It is a curious characteristic of the rough, warlike times in which she lived that she was thrust into prison with her arms and armor, and her barbarous death at Rouen certainly reflects no credit upon the English.

No. 525. *"Washing-Day."* EVERTON SAINSBURY.

No. 141, "*The Haunted Lake*," by Alice
Havers. Among our female artists like Mrs.
Elizabeth Butler, Mrs. E. M. Ward, Louise
Rayner, Linnie Watt, and others, Alice
Havers is entitled to a distinctive position.
Her numerous pictures and designs have
always been marked with good taste as well
as executive ability, and, while she has a
certain power of selection in her subjects,
there is more of nature and less of the
painting-room in her work than we often
meet with in the present day. The motive
of her picture, "*The Haunted Lake*," is self-
suggestive and singularly spontaneous — a
dismal pool, whose deep waters are hidden
away in solitary woods and thick, damp
undergrowth of weeds and trailing plants.
The old wood-cutter, the almost solitary
visitant to such a scene, is pointing out to

No. 590. "*The Betrothal Ring.*"
ARTHUR H. WEIGALL.

two girls, whose exploring footsteps curiosity has led to the spot, the dismal pool, and
doubtless, with the garrulity of age, he is telling them the legend of where the ghost
appears and other nameless horrors, giving to the weird-looking place its title. But,
"uncanny" as the story may be, there are marvelous grace and charm in the pretty maidens,
while the artist has been quick to seize upon and heighten the dramatic effect of her design
by the contrast of youth with the decrepi-
tude of age.

No. 1616. "*Sally in our Alley.*" E. S. KENNEDY.

No. 124, "*Preparations for the Market,
Quimperlé*," and "*A Shop in Quimperlé*,"
are studies in the south of Brittany, by
Stanhope A. Forbes. In No. 124 an old
woman, kneeling by her basket of vegetables and miscellaneous commodities in-
tended for market, is holding a fowl in
her hands as she discusses with her daughter the prices to be asked, and makes other
arrangements. The girl, wearing the pic-

turesque wooden *sabots* of her class, listens, seated upon a hen-coop. The artist appears to have painted his picture on the spot, for the glimpse of the village in the background and the figures of the women are distinctly French. This young artist's pictures attracted attention last year.

In No. 1616, "*Sally in our Alley,*" a quaint old ballad, has furnished the text for E. Sherrard Kennedy's design:

> "On Sunday, dressed in all my best,
> I walk abroad with Sally."

In one of the narrower streets of London of the last century, the young apprentice, clad in gorgeous apparel—a bright-yellow coat of spruce cut—walks out with pretty Sally on his arm, the admired of all beholders. What cares he for mocking gibe and jest, for the old vintner proffering a pot of foaming porter, for the children who ape his proudly contented walk with his sweetheart, or for the thronging crowd around, who laugh, make fun of, and perhaps envy the happy couple? The painter's idea of old London, with its narrow streets, overhanging houses, gabled windows, and swinging oil-lamps, is not badly seen in the present Health Exhibition at South Kensington, in the portion devoted to the imitation of

24 × 36.

No. 149. "*Heads or Tails?*" A. WEIR.

our city in ancient times. But all is strangely altered, and we live now under a rule of law and order. No more do unruly apprentices flock together in the streets at some affront, real or imaginary, to those of their order; and no longer is any class allowed to take the law into its own hands, and show in broils, tumults, and broken heads, defiance of authority and good government. Mr. Kennedy's picture has somewhat of the character of

8

an historical treatise, dealing with scenes and characters in our great city long since passed away; but it is in all respects extremely interesting.

No. 1537. "*A Midway Inn*," by F. W. Lawson. In a quaint, picturesque inn, such as was the "Tabard" or "The Three Nuns" in the olden time, the artist has pictured groups of travelers who might have assembled in a similar edifice in, say, the seventeenth century.

No. 1537. "*A Midway Inn*." F. W. Lawson.

At a table in the foreground on the left, free lances and reckless scoundrels quarrel over their cards. One raises a wine-flagon, while another draws his dagger, and together these desperadoes alarm the house. In the distance a lady seeks the protection of her father, and on the right a frightened child clings to its nurse. Another lady stops, at the wild tumult, as she descends the stairs; and an old man, who rather recalls Gaspard the miser, peers curiously from a gallery in the rear. The landlady, feeling that the honor of her house is at stake, starts, keys in hand, from her cozy corner. But, apart from the brawlers, the tide of life in the old posting-inn goes on: the cook is seen by the glow of the firelight; down a long passage we catch a glimpse of horses; market-people are here from some neighboring village; and the country element is suggested in a "jolly postboy" saluting an apparently by no means reluctant maiden. Then we note in a corner a Jacobite, a courtier of St. Germains, bribing a swashbuckler who drinks success to the cause of "the king over the water," as he takes the golden "*louis d'ors*" of "*Le Roi Soleil*." Full of strong life and quaint sketches of character is this pictured posting-house of the olden days—of the times of Marlborough and Turenne, of Villeroi and Sarsfield, who fought in the open field, and our soldiers followed "Corporal John," and found "glory and plunder but never retreat" in the trenches of some Flemish town or in the pillage of some Rhenish château. The artist, Mr. F. W. Lawson, is one whose life has not been without its vicissitudes. Brother of the

THE VERY IMAGE.

Joseph Clark.

late Cecil G. Lawson, the young landscape-painter whose recent early death we had occasion to regret, he began his artistic career as a designer on wood for various periodicals, and notably "The Graphic." Then followed his series of illustrations of the childish beggar-life of London — the sorry existence of those poor little match-sellers and street Arabs, whose uncertain way of keeping body and soul together must be almost as great a mystery to themselves as it is to the outside public. The artist's well-known "*Children of the Great City,*" "*Imprisoned Spring,*" and "*Dawn,*" the latter representing a poor girl dying in a wretched garret, supported in her brother's arms, while the first gleam of day through the window suggests that other "dawn" to which she is about awakening, were all marked with a feeling of poetical

60 × 48

No. 856. "*Primrose-Day.*"
E. M. Merrick.

pathos. Other artists studying London street-life are Mr. T. B. Kennington, Mrs. Archibald Weir, and Miss E. M. Merrick.

No. 856, "*Primrose-Day.*" Two little street Arabs, one a girl, a flower-seller, is engaged fixing in the button-hole of a shoeless crossing-sweeper the favorite flower of the late Lord Beaconsfield, in wearing which members of the Tory party celebrate the anniversary

47 × 31

No. 818. "*Is Darling lawful?*" Sydney W. Lee.

of that lamented nobleman's death. The design is grotesque enough, when one considers how little the giver and receiver know about the matter.

No. 818. "*Is Dueling lawful?*" by Sydney W. Lee, is rather an amusing design, representing a soldier in red coat, seated over a bowl of punch, with the chaplain of his regiment putting the knotty question to him suggested in the title of the work. The chaplain is of opinion that the question is a difficult one, but he hopes that latitude may be

20 × 25.

No. **208**. "*An East Wind.*" H. Hermer.

granted to soldiers in this particular instance. A soldier and a parson together seem a curiously assorted couple, particularly with such a subject under discussion as that now upon the *tapis*. That a man whose trade is war, and his hope of promotion founded upon deeds of blood, should submit to indignity or insult without at once resenting it, is evidently a proposition the worthy divine can not tackle, and he is, if anything, inclined to concede the point by a semi-evasion like that we have but now referred to. In the great military nations of Europe, where the laws as to dueling are very stringent, an officer in the army is in rather an unfortunate position: for if, when insulted, he resents it in a manner which suggests itself, the law takes cognizance of the fact; whereas, if he does not do so, he is ostracized by all his brother officers.

There is capital character in No. 208, "*An East Wind,*" by Howard Helmick, a study of an old gentleman who certainly is rapidly approaching the "last stage of all that ends this strange eventful history," standing gazing ruefully from the window, as he seeks to explain the twinge of rheumatism in his back by finding that the wind is in that ill-omened quarter—the east. The study of extreme senility in the figure of the old man is mingled —as usual with Mr. Helmick's works—with a strong sense of humor.

Nos. 1554, 1555, and 1556, "*A Love-Story*" ("*The Letter*"—"*A Trial*"—"*Happier than ever*"), by Maria Brooks. Three tableaux in one frame: No. 1, Dolly, the housemaid,

17 × 10.	17 × 12.	17 × 10.
No. 1554.	No. 1555.	No. 1556.
"*The Letter.*"	"*A Trial.*"	"*Happier than ever.*"

"*A Love-Story.*"   MARIA BROOKS.

reading a letter just received; No. 2, poor Dolly seated and in tears over her missive; and No. 3, that fortunate maiden looking the very embodiment of contentment and delight. Of course, a good deal is left to the imagination in this subject. It is difficult to know what has happened in the second tableau to cause such grief. Has Lubin played a practical joke on poor Dolly, and stated in the body of his letter that he no longer loves her, while in a postscript he confesses he has only been having a little fun, and assures her of his undying affection? That appears a not unlikely explanation of this pictured page in the life of a little housemaid, but anyway the subject is cleverly and suggestively treated.

The picture sketched on the next page is one of two clever *genre* subjects by a young artist, to which attention may well be drawn in these pages. They were hung rather out of sight in the Royal Academy, and have been missed altogether by many visitors. The first is "*The Archæologist*," an old gentleman, in eighteenth-century costume, examining some sculpture in a museum; the second "*A Walk with Grandpapa*," remarkable for ease and

No. 120. "*A Walk with Grandpapa.*" H. E. DETMOLD.

close study of character. Mr. Detmold has studied in foreign schools, and is a painter whose work should be looked for in future exhibitions.

No. 386, "*Going to Work.*" This and the two following works are "*Three Scenes in a Miner's Life*," from the brush of A. Dixon:

"'Get up!' the caller calls, 'get up!'
 And in the dead of night
To win the bairns their bite and sup,
 I rise, a weary wight."

In a cottage home a miner, at earliest light of dawn, has risen from his bed, and, safety-lamp in hand, says farewell to his wife and child as he hurries off to his laborious and often dangerous work. The young wife, standing by the window, with all her life bound up in child and husband, thinks not of harm or ill to happen to him she loves so well.

In No. 567, "*To the Rescue*," all is changed. A terrible explosion in the mine, smoke from the pit-mouth, and women, children, and others are flying to the scene in agony of apprehension for the safety of those near and dear to them. Then follows the horror of suspense before those who are but too willing dare attempt to succor those who may yet be living in the dark recesses of the mine. But at length it is pronounced safe, for those anxious to help, to attempt a rescue. The men fearlessly descend into the prison-house; and then, in No. 544, "*Rescued*," we see those happily wrested from the jaws of death. The young wife is there, and,

70 × 50.
No. 386. "*Going to Work.*"

60 × 25.
No. 567. "*To the Rescue.*"

60 × 25.
No. 544. "*Rescued.*"

"*Three Scenes in a Miner's Life.*" A. DIXON.

with a joy and thankfulness too great for utterance, the child clings to her father, and even the dog fawns upon his master as he licks his hand. Such are the stirring passages in the life of the laborer in mines. But this is only one side of the picture; the other we dare not touch upon, for it is harrowing in its details, and the despair of those whose fate it is to look no more upon the living is perhaps suggested by contrast in the happiness of the

No. 795. *"Wishes and Fishes."* WILSON GROSSMITH.

"All things come to those who wait."

No. 24. *"Artists."* ROBERT FOWLER.

No. 1541. *"The Last Mile."* R. COLLINSON.

favored, whose brighter story is seen in the picture of the "*Rescued*" we have but now referred to.

No. 795, "*Wishes and Fishes*" ("All things come to those who wait"), by Weedon Grossmith, is, properly speaking, portraiture in costume of half a century ago. A boy and girl, a pair of Izaak Waltonians, are patiently fishing on the sedgy bank of a river. The little folk look both pretty and picturesque, with much childish grace about their figures, but, truth to speak, they are anything but keen anglers, and appear weary of non-success. Let us hope that the quotation in the text will come true, so that patience may meet with its reward.

No. 24, "*Artists*," by Robert Fowler. Two very graceful female figures, one seated, regarding a canvas upon the easel, which is placed out in the open air. The design is just sufficiently obscure to make it interesting. Are these beautiful girls—for they really are alto-gether charming in their light, silvery draperies and red head-dresses—themselves professors of palette and brushes, or are they only artists in taste, feeling, and appreciation of art? There is nice symbolism in the motive of the work, and so much grace in the conception and composition that one is quite content to take the picture with all its little half-suggested doubts, and accept it gratefully for the sense of beauty it arouses in the mind.

In No. 1541, "*The Last Mile*," by Robert Collinson, we see a good old dame, appar-ently a villager of the humblest class, who has been tramping wearily along the road until she reaches a mile-stone, happily the last before she reaches her destination. Life's load of years not being sufficient, she has to carry a bundle, containing possibly all her worldly goods, and this she has placed upon the ground as she rests her-self while attempting to decipher, upon the hard stone, the distance yet to be traversed ere the feeble footsteps will bring her to shelter and re-pose. Fields and foliage look young and bright and beautiful, in strong contrast to the venerable life which now, like the stone the poor old lady is consulting, indicates the last stage of the journey.

No. 311, "*The Quarrel*," by C. W. Pittard.

"Here's much to do with hate, but more with love."

Here, again, the subject is one full of suggestion. A young lady, richly robed in pink satin, is seated

No. 311. "*The Quarrel.*" C. W. PITTARD.

in a chair, anger in her face and mien. Behind her stands a young cavalier, crushing his
broad-leaved hat in one hand, while the other is fiercely closed. Upon the floor, at the
lady's feet, lie some flowers, which have evidently been thrown there in scorn and disgust.
What has occasioned this dire disturbance, what has aroused the hate, which, as Shakespeare
says, is so near akin to love, between the pair? It is to be presumed that they are lovers,
and, if that be so, "*Amantium iræ amoris integratiovest*," and, shortly, their love will be the
stronger for this passing anger. But, meantime, the social atmosphere is disturbed. The
flowers—those pretty love-tokens, suggestive of beauty, peace, and happiness—are fiercely
cast away, and their at one time loving donor is considered almost as a foe. So much for
the passion of love and its strange vicissitudes.

No. 646. "*Cook's Straits, New Zealand.*" NICOLAS CHEVALIER.

No. 646, "*Cook's Straits, New Zealand*," by Nicolas Chevalier, is a departure in art, on
the part of this painter, from subjects we are accustomed to from his brush. With Eastern
scenes, views in Cairo, and elsewhere, we are all familiar, but, like Luke Fildes and other
of our more enterprising artists, he has exercised his genius in striking out a new path for
himself with considerable success. M. Chevalier's pictures always exhibit great care and
technical completeness.

No. 95, "*For those in Peril on the Sea*," by Jessie Macgregor. The painter, a young
artist of considerable promise, made her *début* a few seasons since with her picture illustrating in three tableaux the quaint old ballad of "The Mistletoe-Bough." This she followed
in succeeding years with works of more or less promise, until the production of her present
picture. In an old wainscoted chamber, whose large window opens out upon the sea, a
family group is assembled. Either it is evening, or the apartment is darkened by the rag-
ing storm, and two girls are singing to the accompaniment of a third at the piano. One

little fellow, too young to be conscious of impending evil, is engaged with his toys upon the floor, and a servant holds at the window a child who looks out upon the angry ocean. As far as the sentiment of the picture is concerned, it matters not whether the singers carol

No. 95. *"For those in Peril on the Sea."* JESSIE MACGREGOR.

plaintively of danger to those near and dear to them, or, taking a deeper, wider view, whisper in sweet melody a prayer for the safety of all those "who go down to the deep in ships." The grandeur and solemnity of the war of elements in a storm are amply realized in the darkened atmosphere seen from the window and in the saddened faces of the hymn-singers.

No. 499, "*The Herring-Harvest,*" by John White, is a characteristic study of a fishing-village, with a fisherman selling his store of herrings from the panniers with which his donkey is laden. At a fisherman's cottage, on the right of the picture, children are also amusing themselves with the fish, which, during this season of plenty, form their staple article of food. The street is a curious, winding one, with those remarkably primitive cottages, half mud, half plaster, one is accustomed to see in such villages.

No. 1615, "*A Yarmouth Row,*" by Percy R. Craft, is in some respects not dissimilar in motive from the last-named subject — only that Yarmouth is, as we are aware, a place of importance on the east coast of Eng-

No. 499. "*The Herring-Harvest.*" JOHN WHITE.

Land. The houses in this picture, while they are quite as picturesque—oddly-shaped, with pointed roofs and other individual peculiarities—are altogether larger, and form indeed the

No. 1615. "A Yarmouth Row." P. R. Craft.

leading motive of the design. Of all the large towns on the Norfolk coast there is, perhaps, not one which has more completely retained its ancient character than Yarmouth—

some of the streets, like the one in our illustration, almost reminding us of some of the curious old wynds of Edinburgh. The town of Yarmouth is as much the resort of the middle and lower classes for sea-bathing as Brighton, in the south of England, is for those of a somewhat higher position socially. Yarmouth is also a popular sketching-ground for artists, who are never weary of delineating the Yare, the fishing-boats, and steam-tugs, together with the more prominent points of interest upon the coast with which the district certainly abounds.

54 × 34.

No. 715. *"St. Agnes, of the Early Christian Martyrs."* JAMES ARCHER.

Mr. James Archer, a member of the Scottish Academy, a painter who has been an exhibitor for many years, painting both subject-pictures and portraits, sent this year two pictures to the Royal Academy. The first is an elaborate composition representing the martyrdom of St. Agnes; the second, entitled *"You a Christian!"* A young pagan lover discovers a cross worn by his betrothed, and starts back with the exclamation "You a Christian!" There are much learning and evident painstaking in these two pictures; but Mr. Archer's portraits, notably one lately painted of Professor Blackie, show his powers to the best advantage.

No. 1653, *"Vespers,"* by F. D. Hardy. The subject introduces us to monastic life; not the phase of monkish existence in which our well-known young painter, Mr. Dendy Sadler,

delights, and which he delineates with such keen humor—the sly indulgence of the worthy
fathers in the good things of this life, their preference for pastimes like fishing, etc., to pen-
ance, or similar scenes—but a group of monks in the belfry, ringing in their brethren to
service. They are shut off from the interior of the church, which is to be seen in the background, by a curtain screen, which one of their number is closing. Probably their present

No. 1653. *"Vespers."* F. D. Hardy.

occupation is not quite so distasteful to them as digging their own graves, kneeling all
night upon the cold stones of the chapel, fasting, or other like cheerful modes of passing
away their time with which they are credited by historical record. Still, the view of life is a
curious one, when we see the grave and learned doing the work of menials; the self-evident
object of existence as social beings cast aside for self-denials which are opposed to nature,
and are not demanded by law, Scripture, or common sense. Many of the monks in the olden
time, like Fra Angelico and Bartolommeo, were splendid artists, and made their age illustri-

ous by their works, or, like Savonarola and Martin Luther, were pioneers in a revolution of truth; but modern professors of this curious system of self-sacrifice appear to do little else

No. 300. "*Caught Tripping.*" A. W. BAYES.

than fritter away the great boon of life in useless observances and customs, doing no good to the great human family of which they form a part. In saying this much, however, we say nothing against Mr. Hardy's picture, which is not only excellent in scenic effect, but also as a study of character.

No. 714. "'*Mong the Thick-falling Dew.*" EDGAR WILLS.

No. 300, "*Caught Tripping*," by A. W. Bayes. Here the scene presented to us is that of a Puritan's household. The master of the house, evidently a staunch non-conformist, with steeple-crowned hat and clothes of somber shade, has been away from home, and now is returning, Bible in hand, opens the door, when, dreadful to relate, he finds his three daughters—prim lassies in white caps and gray dresses—engaged, the one dancing while the others are approving spectators of the performance! Had they only been engaged in sewing, or reading "the good book," all might have been well, but this exhibition of natural feeling in the young is really too shocking. The dancer trips it merrily, and looks charming in her primly modest costume. We may imagine the *dénoûment*, the righteous wrath of the old Puritan, and the sound lecturing the young sinners will get before they are con-

sidered purged of their wickedness. Technically, the design is full of merit, the incident being fully told, and most amusingly.

No. 714, "*'Mong the Thick-falling Dews*," by Edgar Wills. A pleasant pastoral, with cattle in the eventide settling to rest among the thick grasses of pasture-land near the margin of some water. The time appointed for Nature's rest approaches, and in the gathering gloom the group of cows—animals so specially typical of peaceful industry—forms a natural and suggestive adjunct to such a scene.

No. 574, "*A Side-Glance*," by G. Crosland Robinson.

16 × 13.

No. 574. "*A Side-Glance*."

G. C. Robinson.

"She gives a side-glance and looks down—
Beware!"

A study of a bright, pleasant-looking girl, who glances downward to the left. As regards the original of the picture, the warning in the quotation may not be without its value to the more impressionable of the opposite sex.

No. 698, "*The Young Squire*," by Francis S. Walker. In the corner of an orchard the young gentleman who forms the motive of the work is stretched at his ease full length upon the grass, amusing himself for the fleeting hour chatting to two girls. The maidens are not, we should imagine, of exactly the same sphere of life as the squire, and they appear to be looking at him as quite a superior being. Of course the damsels, pretty and innocent-looking as they are, may have that shrewd common sense and commercial instinct enabling them to see in a young, handsome, and wealthy gentleman not at all a bad match, matrimonially speaking. But it is quite certain, even if he has any thought of settling for life, that he can not, according to the laws of England, marry both of them, and to select either one or the other would arouse horrible jealousy and heart-burning. Besides, it is not at all unusual for young squires to see a great many pretty girls, and have no other thought than whiling away a passing hour or so in agreeable flirtation. But we wish them well, for they certainly form a picturesque and charming group.

No. 698. "*The Young Squire.*" F. S. WALKER.

In No. 329, "*Ludgate Hill*, 1883," the artist, C. J. Watson, illustrates one of the busiest centers of the British metropolis, and one of the five great roadways of traffic branching off from the basilica of St. Paul's. The cathedral, a peep of which is obtained in the picture, is second only in size to St. Peter's at Rome, and has ever been held by those versed in ecclesiastical architecture to be even more symmetrical and of juster proportions than the colossal edifice in the Eternal City. The latter building has, however, the advantage in that, while the fine site where it is situated is kept comparatively open and free, St. Paul's is unfortunately dwarfed by the close proximity of surrounding warehouses, which scarcely permit the ordinary passenger the opportunity of judging of the architectural beauties of the grand old cathedral.

The garden of a pretty country house, with clustering ivy, honeysuckle, and other trailing plants, and two girls, one seated, the other reading a letter as she thoughtfully paces

No. 329. *"Langton Hall,*
1883." C. J. Watson.

along the walk, has formed the subject for a picture which the artist, Arthur L. Vernon, calls *"It might have been"* (No. 123). We are led to imagine that the young lady is reading in her just-received missive of the marriage of a former admirer, and we must also suppose she reads the announcement with some regret. She is, however, still young enough and pretty enough to lead one to hope that there may be a solace for disappointed love in store for her, so that her future path in life may not be an altogether solitary one.

No. 26, *"The Pathos of Life,"* by R. G. Hutchison.

"Pale Death knocks with impartial hand
At prince's hall and peasant's hut."

In one of the curious, cupboard-like beds that we occasionally meet with in a country cottage, a peasant, the father and bread-winner for the family, lies dying. His figure is not seen in the picture, but the story is most graphically told, and he is surely there. Bowed down in grief, his wife kneels upon the floor, and his aged mother leans against the side of the bed. The children, scarce appreciating the magnitude of their disaster, are yet hushed and somewhat frightened, and desist from play. The artist touches with a poet's feeling upon the lights and shadows of life, and in this design pictures pathetically the universal empire of the dread foe to whom both prince and peasant must at last succumb.

No. 1618, *"Hickory Dickory Dock,"* by Edith Hipkins, is a pleasant study of a young mother holding her little child up to the clock, while she repeats the old nursery rhyme. Miss Hipkins, who is steadily improving in her art, has cleverly availed herself of the attractive sentiment of motherhood in this nice little work.

No. 312, *"Meditation,"* by A. Glendening, Jr. A rather spruce maiden in quilted skirt, and wearing a coquettish little cap, has found her way to a corner of the garden, where, sitting down, with love-letter in her lap, she resigns herself to her thoughts. What those thoughts may be is

No. 123. *"It might have been."*
A. L. Vernon.

THE DECLARATION OF WAR.
J. D. Linton.

No. 26. "*The Pathos of Life.*" R. G. HUTCHISON.

left to the spectator to determine, but they evidently are not sad ones, and all will wish so pretty a lass a happy fate.

No. 240, "*A Ramsay Wrecker,*" by J. H. E. Partington. A wild sea, scarce settled down from recent storm, a stiffish gale blowing, and rain, with a good, strong-built fisher lass, loaded with wreckage which she is conveying along the sands to her home, are the ingredients from which Mr. Partington has constructed a clever picture. The girl has not made much of a "haul," however, her prize apparently consisting principally of planks from the ill-fated ship. But she seems to be content, and has probably loaded herself to the extent of her power. The receding tide appears to show in the distance a vessel which has

No. 1618. "*Hickory Dickory Dock.*" F. HOPKINS.

No. 312. "*Meditation.*" ALFRED GLENDENING, JR.

fixed ill upon the treacherous sands, and it is possibly from that source the fair wrecker secures her spoil. She is barefoot, and in her evident physical strength looks not ungraceful.

No. 1524, "*Expectation*," by G. Hillyard Swinstead. A pastoral subject, with barefooted country girl making her way from her father's cottage, followed by those who are evidently her pensioners, some geese and a calf. The creatures, fearless where they have ever met with kindness, seek from her hand the food to which they are accustomed. This charming little picture is nice in design, scheme of color, and general effect. In the white geese the artist has embodied, while he has carried much further, the rudimentary principle of coloring that everything harmonizes with white.

Another work from the same hand, No. 1582, without title, but with the quotation—

"Oh! merry goes the time when the heart is young,
For Paris gives the pippin for the best song sung"—

No. 240. "*A Ramsay Wrecker*,"
J. H. E. PARTINGTON.

is rather Watteau-like in motive, and very different from the design we have but now referred to. Here we see a group of ladies and gentlemen who, having selected a shady spot under some trees, are indulging in a little *siesta* or picnic upon the greensward. Careless and young, when the heart is fresh and life is in its spring-time, the group reposes in joyous ease, and makes merry with music and laughter. Nor have the merry-makers forgotten creature comforts, as the viands spread upon their impromptu table testify.

In No. 313, "*Circe*," the artist, H. M. Paget, presents to us the beautiful enchantress and daughter of Sol seated at her loom with a tiger at her side. One can hardly suppose that the fell sorceress, who worked such woe to the unhappy companions of Ulysses in turning them into swine, or behaved with no less cruelty to Scylla and others, is here engaged weaving her mischievous spells, for she looks quite contemplative, and very graceful and pretty.

No. 91, "*Quiet Hours*," by Percy Bigland. A capital study of a young fish-wife, seated in a kind of balcony of her house, in a quaint old Flemish fishing-village, while her goodman is away upon the seas. She has thrown off her sabots for greater comfort, and looks quiet and contemplative as her busy fingers ply the knitting-needles. Her face is of that better-class type, where the characteristics of her race are sufficiently and yet not too prominently marked. Her needs in this life are few, and those probably supplied in the humblest fashion; and yet she looks the very picture of contentment and happiness.

No. 145, "*When the Long Days are ended*," by W. Frank Calderon. The artist, who is the son of Mr. Calderon, the Academician, adopts an entirely different *rôle* of art from his

No. 1524. "*Expectation*." G. H. SWINSTEAD.

father. But, in another way, his designs have sentiment, and are strong in their adherence to nature. In the picture before us (page 80) a wagoner brings down his team of horses to drink in the shallow part of a stream. The labors of the day are over, and the wearied beasts lave their bodies in the cool waters. The sky is brilliant in the light of the departing sun, and the whole scene suggests the time of coming quiet and rest.

There is a character of bright life and sunshine in H. Tuck's "*A Corner of the Hay-*

field," No. 813, that carries with it a peculiar charm. The new-mown hay lies thick upon the meadows, and the hay-makers are busy at their task loading the wagons with Nature's

No. 1582. *"Oh! merry goes the time when the heart is young,*
For Paris gives the pippin for the best song sung." G. H. SWINSTEAD.

summer harvest. The hay-field and its calm, joyous associations have ever been a theme of special interest with the English artist. In sylvan subjects the painters of France have, as a rule, preferred more dramatic designs, or those in which the sad element predominates, as

No. 313. *"Circe."* H. M. PAGET.

we find in their aged wood-cutters or weary laborers, while in colder latitudes and more sterile countries, like Russia, works of this class appear to have had little or no hold upon the imaginations of the people. But with English artists the hay-field has certainly ever been a fruitful source of inspiration.

No. 509, "*To Anthea*," by G. C. Hindley. An exceedingly vigorous and spirited design, in which the principal figure is a gentleman, who, having thrown off his shoes and cast his

No. 91. "*Quiet Hours.*" PERCY BIGLAND.

rapier upon the ground, pens his missive to his lady. Her portrait is upon the table before him, and, whether inspired by that or by more tender recollections, certain it is that face and figure testify to the writer's earnestness of purpose. A friend, appearing upon the scene, presses back the arras as he enters the apartment.

In the second picture by this artist, No. 195, "*The Standard-Bearer*," the study is chiefly

No. 145. "*When the Long Days are ended.*" W. F. CALDERON.

No. 813. "*A Corner of the Hay-field—Les Foins.*" H. TUCK.

an exercise in character and color. The face, if we mistake not, expresses firm resolve and inflexible will, so that he who in battle would rob him of his sacred trust can only hope to do so either when life has fled or all power of resistance is beaten down.

No. 29, "*I'm for the Ferry*," by Frank E. Cox. A young gleaner, whose armful of corn shows that she has been diligent, is here pictured waiting at the river-side for the ferry-boat. Bronzed by the sun and with somewhat wearied gait, for the girl has doubtless toiled the long day through to earn the little bread of which she is now assured, she seeks her home. It requires no imagination to picture how poor and humble that home must

No. 509. "*To Antlers.*" G. C. Hindley.

be, for it is but the poorest who are driven to so precarious a means of obtaining a scanty meal. Mr. Cox, in his picture, with peculiar grace, teaches a lesson in the history of the laboring poor, and fails not to arouse in the mind a feeling of sympathy which is near akin to charity.

No. 229, "*Africa*," by Thomas Hill, pictures some fruit-sellers with their store of melons and oranges, together with vegetables, arranged in baskets for sale. As a study of character, the design is powerful, the calm and somewhat dignified composure of these people as they quietly wait for customers, and the hot and glowing atmosphere of Africa, being excellently rendered.

No. 908. *"Ruth,"* by S. J. Solomon.

" And Ruth said, ' Entreat me not to leave thee, or to return from following after thee.'"

One of the most pathetic stories of the Bible is here beautifully illustrated by the artist. The moment selected for illustration is when Ruth, clinging to the one she loved so well,

No. 195.　*" The Standard-Bearer,"*　G. C. Hinsley.

uttered the beautiful words quoted above. The scheme of color in the picture is very delicate, and the light draperies are in pleasant harmony with the bright Eastern atmosphere and sky.

The first among English animal-painters is Mr. Briton Rivière, the painter of *"Circe,"* and of *"Daniel in the Lions' Den,"* familiar to us in countless engravings. This painter, who stands to the present generation in the place of Landseer, is an earnest and highly educated worker, aiming at a higher level intellectually than most painters who devote themselves to the portrayal of animal life. In Sir Edwin Landseer's works, one of the principal attractions was the human interest and character with which he endowed the brute creation; in Mr. Rivière's pictures (excepting, perhaps, in his "*Circe*") his animals

No. 29.   "*I'm for the Ferry.*"   F. E. Cox.

seem to live and move as in nature. In "*The King and his Satellites,*" sketched on page 84, there is, as a critic well remarks, "no departure either from leonine or jackal nature, and yet the simple incident of the colossal brute stalking onward, with his abject clients at his heels, who would gladly devour him had they the chance, tells a story eloquently." Nothing that Mr. Rivière has painted, since the pictures we have referred to, will interest more than his "*Lion and Jackals,*" which is now doubtless in the hands of the engraver.

In another subject, "*Actæon*" attacked by dogs, an upright picture, the interest is centered more in landscape; but in "*The Eve of St. Bartholomew*" we have another composition which is far more popular. In spite of this, Mr. Rivière's natural bent is to paint classical and idealistic subjects, and we may yet see many works of imagination from his hand.

No. 229. *"Africa."* THOMAS HILL.

No. 908. *"Ruth."* S. J. SOLOMON.

There are four pictures in the Academy by the veteran animal-painter, T. Sidney Cooper, R.A., one of which, cows on the banks of the Thames, near Tilbury Fort, measures about eleven by seven and a half feet; also four by Richard Ansdell, R.A. Industrious as ever, but failing in health, Mr. Ansdell sends year after year his favorite studies of sheep in the Highlands of Scotland; also scenes from the south of Spain, with mules with their gay trappings, Spanish peasants, and scenery near the Alhambra. Mr. Ansdell has an estate in the north of Scotland, and many of the animals in his pictures are portraits from life.

No. 88. *"The King and his Satellites."* BRITON RIVIÈRE, R.A.

55 × 47.

No. 52. *"The Eve of St. Bartholomew."*

BRITON RIVIÈRE, R. A.

57½ × 41½.

No. 1611. *"Spring: Isle of Skye."*

R. ANSDELL, R. A.

Since Sir Edwin Landseer and Mr. Ansdell began to paint, and to interest the public in Highland scenes, a new generation of animal and landscape painters crowds the walls of the Academy with large canvases. Among the most important and successful of these is Mr. H. W. B. Davis, R. A., one of whose pictures of cattle is sketched below. The interest of this picture is great in landscape, in the color of the hills, and in the wide, open-air

48 × 84.

No. 286. *"On the Hill-side, clearing after Rain."* H. W. B. DAVIS, R. A.

effect which the painter has rendered with great truthfulness and beauty. But this artist's cattle should always be noticed for the close study of nature in every movement, and for the almost monumental or sculpturesque character which he gives to his animals. Mr. Davis was educated as a sculptor, and the value of this early training is generally evident. In 1876 he sent to the Academy a large picture of "*Mares and Foals*," and in 1877 a picture called "*Contentment*"—two oxen by the sea-shore—in both of which the exceptionally fine grouping of animals was observed.

No. 691. "*The Rear-Guard.*" HEYWOOD HARDY.

With Mr. Davis we should naturally mention another painter of the same scenes, Mr. Peter Graham, R. A., whose Scotch cattle, wandering between mist-covered hills, are perhaps even better known; but we must refer to his work in speaking of landscape.

A very interesting animal as well as *genre* painter should be mentioned here; one closely allied to Mr. Rivière in selection of subjects, such as dogs and children in friendly relations, is Mr. Heywood Hardy. His studies of animals, lately published as etchings, heads of lions, horses, etc., are popular in the print-shops, and every year his pictures are on the Academy walls. For the last year he has been living in France, and has sent home some admirable studies of French horse-soldiers. The "rear-guard" of dragoons riding up a quiet road in Brittany, in rather free-and-easy fashion; the last man, saluting a peasant-girl leading a cow by a string, has an air of *vraisemblance* seldom achieved. Mr. Hardy gives exact

No. 739.   *"Sale of Cavalry-Horses in France."*   HEYWOOD HARDY.

portraits of the style and accoutrements of the men: they *"sit on their horses"* unmistakably, the road is a French road, and there are ease of manner and an open-air effect which are so often missed in similar subjects. All this we may see in the foregoing sketch, which Mr. Hardy has made for us; also in the spirited drawing of the central figure in his second

34 × 61.

No. 615. *"Changing Pasture on the Roman Campagna."* R. BEAVIS.

picture, "*The Sale of Cavalry-Horses*," a dragoon, in undress, riding through the fair. The large annual sales of horses in the interior of Brittany are great opportunities for artists. They are held at stated times at Carhaix and other towns easily reached from Paris; also at Pont Aven, where a little colony of French and American students work during the summer months.

Probably no one can paint horses much better at the present time than Mr. R. Beavis, an artist who has been before the public for many years without receiving any special rec-

14 × 16.

No. 597. *"The Orphans."* S. E. WALLER.

ognition from the Academy. He has a wide range of subjects—historical, marine, and pastoral—from studies in Italy, France, Holland, and England. Mr. Beavis paints in oils and water-colors, and last year sent to the Society of Painters in Water-Colors a study of horses under trees near Fontainebleau that indicated his special power as an animal-painter.

One of the most prominent of the young painters in this branch of art is Mr. S. E. Waller. He is very successful in the technique of his art, owing much to the advice

"*The Leader of the Team.*"

E. B. STANLEY MONTEFIORE.

of his friend Briton Rivière. For a comparatively young artist his work is excellent, and, should he succeed in maintaining his present progress, it is not difficult to foretell his attainment in the future to academic honors. The artist's wife, Mrs. Mary L. Waller, is a portrait-painter, and contributed "*Mildred, Daughter of Colonel Tryon,*" to the present exhibition. Mr. Waller's painting of "*The Orphans*" represents a couple of deer in a park, which a young lady, who is kneeling in the snow, is feeding from a basket.

Another young painter of promise is Mr. E. S. Montefiore, whose picture of "*Leaving Labor,*" horses in a field (his first important picture in the Academy), was a success last year. "*The Leader of the Team*" is well indicated in the accompanying sketch by the artist.

Mr. Emms has chosen a popular subject in the three noble St. Bernard dogs, who, having returned from their trained mission of mercy in the snow, are now waiting admittance at the monastery-door. Sent out by the monks, and provided with flasks and other means of succor for those luckless travelers who may have been overwhelmed in deep snow-drifts in the dangerous mountain defiles, the grand brutes, with an all but human instinct, have fulfilled their duty, and now seek for readmittance and shelter. Without being able to sympathize with the cynical asceticism of Lord Byron, in his lines—

"I never had a friend but one,
And there he lies "—

upon the tomb of his favorite, at Newstead, there is not, perhaps, in the animal creation anything with the sagacity, the intelligence, and the unselfish affection of the dog. Starve and maltreat your canine follower, as did Mr. Bill Sykes of happy memory, still he will be faithful to you. Call upon his intelligence in a

No. 248. "*The Return to the Monastery.*"

JOHN EMMS.

12

7 × 9

No. 598. *"The Cottage-Door."* W. B. Baird.

manner scarcely to be credited, as in the case of the Scotch collie in charge of his flock, and he will respond; or venture upon personal chastisement with the most deadly and dangerous of his kind, as did Charlotte Brontë with her formidable bull-dog, and he will submit. Faithful, stanch, and true, of all domestic animals commend us to the dog.

No. 598, *"The Cottage-Door,"* by W. B. Baird, is a group of household pets that appeals to the sympathies of man in another way, in that it is ornamental and also edible. Dogs are *not* eaten, at least not in civilized countries. Mr. Baird pictures a hen with her brood of chicks on the cottage door-step. In Ireland it would be the pig that would be

40 × 60

No. 324. *"The Gillie's Kitchen,"* J. S. Noble.

No. 845. *"The Squire's Pets."* FRANK DICEY.

the courted and familiar companion; while in Great Britain the humblest cottage is not without that ornamental, useful, and tasty luxury, the fowl.

No. 324. *"The Gillie's Kitchen,"* by J. S. Noble, pictures the spoils of the chase in the body of a fine stag and other game, together with a blood-hound and a deer-hound. Capital in texture, the artist is also particularly apt in the composition of his pictures. It is a difficult thing to *fall* gracefully, but Mr. Noble's animals always *fall* well, and the group before us is capitally arranged, the pen-and-ink sketch indicating the lines of composition with unusual exactness.

No. 391. *"Caught at last: Retribution."* WALTER HUNT.

No. 845, "*The Squire's Pets*," by Frank Dicey. In the breakfast-room of an ancient mansion is assembled a group consisting of the squire, his daughter, and a brace of handsome hounds. There is a *double entendre* in the title, for doubtless the lovely girl, who stands holding in her hand a dainty morsel for one or other of the expectant favorites, is

No. 1613.　"*Steerage-Passengers.*"　J. YATES CARRINGTON.

as much a *pet* with the owner of the house, who sits at the great fireplace reading his newspaper, as the dogs who have contributed their best to many a good day's sport. The animals turn their heads up wistfully toward their young mistress, and, being well-bred dogs, as becomes the followers of an ancient house, they do not fawn or jump up, but await in silence the expected favor. Mr. Dicey is a skillful portrait-painter, and we rather imagine that the subject is altogether portraiture; and, if so, the artist has woven his design into an exceedingly interesting little scene of domestic life.

No. 391, "*Caught at last: Retribution*," by Walter Hunt, is an amusing and suggestive incident in animal life. Stealthily, as is his wont, a fox has stolen down upon the sheep-fold and, the shepherd being absent, has made prey of a little lamb. But the brigand meets with his punishment in the very moment of success; for, scarcely has he had time to seize upon and kill his little victim, ere the trusty sheep-dog—possibly alarmed by the bleating of the fold—appears upon the scene, and, seizing Reynard *flagrante delicto*, he at once administers condign punishment and lays the marauder dead upon the field. There is here capital opportunity for the delineation of animal character. The distant sheep, strong it is true, but, fortunately for man, proverbially timid and unconscious of the way in which to apply their strength; the slaughtered lamb and his dead destroyer, with the active

38 × 26.

No. 1571. *"Fatal Fidelity."* F. M. Cox.

and handsome collie, panting with the exertion of his victory, standing triumphant as he looks anxiously toward his approaching master, form together a most effective and telling design.

These are works which become very popular as engravings, and in every year's exhibi-

tion of the Academy some painter achieves success by a happily chosen subject. Thus Mr.
Edwin Douglas, with his graceful pictures of Jersey cows and maidens, and Mr. C. Burton-
Barber, with his dogs and children, have become widely known.

No. 252. "*Oxford, from Iffley.*"　VICAT COLE, R. A.

Other animal-painters whose names should be mentioned are Mr. Bouverie Goddard, the
painter of "*Lord Wolverton's Blood-hounds*"; Mr. Samuel Carter, the painter of "*Herne, the
Hunter*"; Mr. John Charlton; Mr. J. Yates Carrington; Mr. J. T. Nettleship, who sent a
large picture of a lioness and cub just saved from drowning; and Mr. Blinks, whose
"*Victory*" is sketched on page xiii.

No. 1571, "*Fatal Fidelity,*" by E. Morant Cox. A capital and very suggestive incident
excellently told. During the Civil Wars some of the Parliamentarian troops have lighted
upon the mansion of a Cavalier, which they are about despoiling, but, before doing
so, they make eager search for the master of the house. He, however, is securely
hidden away, and might have escaped in safety, but for the too faithful attachment of his
little spaniel dog, which, having run away from his mistress, flies at once to the wainscot,
where, behind some sliding-panels, his master is secreted, and there stands whining and beg-
ging for admission. This is not lost upon the pursuers, who at once guess the meaning of
the animal's importunity, and, while some of them hasten to avail themselves of the clew

LA COCARDE TRICOLORE. PARIS, 1789.

G. P. Jacomb-Hood.

thus afforded, others seize upon the lady of the house, who in wild alarm is descending the staircase with the view of recalling the dog to her side. But it is now too late, and the faithful animal, all unwittingly, has betrayed his master to his foes.

Of the painters of mountains, river, and sea, artists who devote themselves almost entirely to Nature and live for the most part in the midst of the scenes they depict, there is a larger number in England every year. There are the artists who chiefly study the Thames, like Vicat Cole, Keeley Halswelle, Alfred Parsons, and W. L. Wyllie; others who are more at home on the mountains, like Peter Graham, J. McWhirter, A. R. A., and C. G. Johnson; others, again, who work on the sea-coast, like J. C. Hook, R. A., John Brett, A. R. A., Hamilton Macallum, C. N. Hemy, G. A. Waterlow; and others who, like Henry Moore, work actually out at sea in rough and windy weather. We can do little more than indicate in these pages, by means of sketches by the artists, the subjects and styles of some prominent landscapists. Without color, a verbal description of many landscapes might prove uninteresting.

The principal picture by Vicat Cole, R. A., who is painting a series of views of the river Thames "from its source to the sea," was a view outside the cathedral city of Oxford, seen

No. 257. *"A Gleam of the Setting Sun."* KEELEY HALSWELLE.

under sunshine, with the green foliage of early summer. Two other pictures by him were painted at Bisham and Mapledurham Lock. The rich, sleepy aspect of pasture-land, near the upper reaches of the Thames, where the water is kept up at all seasons by means of locks, and often overflows the meadows, is indicated in Mr. Cole's sketch. We have only to picture to ourselves the bright, fresh green of the fields, the dark-brown stems of the oaks and elms, and the gray willows on the banks, "with their feet in the water," the hay-makers at work, and the sheep at rest by the road-side, to realize the landscape of Constable and Gainsborough—the source of inspiration of Goldsmith and Gray.

All down the river, between Oxford and Maidenhead, in these modern days, the artist's "house-boat" is to be seen, generally moored in some cozy corner, half hidden among the

No. 902. "*The Ploughman homeward plods his Weary Way.*" B. W. LEADER, A. R. A.

trees. This is the new method of work, a house and studio afloat giving opportunities for a closer study of nature than working on shore.

Here Mr. Keeley Halswelle lived for several summers, and painted the series of studies of the Thames which formed a separate exhibition in London last season. Mr. Halswelle is an almost unique example of a successful figure-painter abandoning figures altogether and painting landscape pure and simple. His landscapes are most carefully planned with this idea; the balance of parts is so perfect that a figure introduced even in the distance would injure the composition. The floating beds of water-lilies people the landscape and endow it with almost human interest.

Many other painters of the upper Thames we might mention here. Some artists, like

Mr. G. D. Leslie, R.A., have houses near its banks. Last season Mr. Leslie sent to the Academy a charming picture called "*Thames Roses*"—a girl in a boat-house seated by the river; also another small picture of three figures at Benson Ferry. We mention Mr. G. D. Leslie's name here because his work has an old English quaintness and color which har-

80 × 50.

No. 558. "*The Vale of Light.*" ERNEST PARTON.

monize well with these surroundings. This is the landscape which Mr. Alfred Parsons and Mr. Abbey have made so familiar in book-illustration, fascinating scenery which we hardly care to leave for the flat lands, for woods, mountains, and sea, where so many artists take us in their pictures.

Mr. J. C. Hook, R.A., and Mr. J. W. Oakes, A.R.A., both veteran painters of sea and

24 × 39.

No. 1621.   "*Where the Wild Grass fringes the Forest.*"   VAL DAVIS.

landscape, contribute annually many important works.   Mr. B. W. Leader, A. R. A., paints flat land under sunset with poetic feeling; the land of Crome it might be, but in reality not far from his home at Worcester in the midland counties.   In the paintings of Vicat Cole

30 × 51.

No. 325.   "*Cut off by the Floods.*"   FLITCROFT FLETCHER.

and Leader there is more consideration given to composition than in the work of many of the prominent landscape artists. Leader in his fine work showing the plowman's team returning in the evening light, and the old village church-spire rising sharp against the sky, has been compared to Herr Heffner and some painters of the French school; but in the English landscapes of the old school the first thought is generally local accuracy, the second the sentiment to be conveyed.

Perhaps Mr. Ernest Parton's poetic *"Vale of Light"* (558), which hung in the center of the fifth gallery, may have more in common with the school of impressionists; and we may see in the sketches in these pages evidence of much poetic sentiment and even high ambition in this branch of art. There are beauty and suggestiveness in the silence of Mr. Val Davis's *"Where the Wild Grass fringes the Forest,"* with the little white calf standing by a pool; close the eyes a little, when looking at the sketch, and you will get the effect of this picture; better, also, of Mr. Flitcroft Fletcher's *"Cut off by the Floods"* (325). *"My Love has gone a-sailing"* is the work of a young Scotchman, which has been purchased for "a possession forever" by the Council of the Royal Academy. The small sketch, by David Murray (on page 105), will serve to identify the picture, which has fine qualities if it is not a great example of landscape art.

Mr. McWhirter, A. R. A., is a figure as well as landscape painter, but this year — as a few years ago, when he painted a single birch-tree, called *"The Lady of the Woods"*—he has given a view near Edinburgh, looking from the heights

No. 491. *"The Windings of the Forth."*
J. McWhirter, A. R. A.

over the river Forth, in which fir-trees take the place of figures and form an important part of the subject. This was Mr. McWhirter's principal picture of the year.

There are much feeling for composition and breadth of effect in the landscapes by Mr. C. E. Johnson, who is, at the same time, a close student of nature. The lovely banks of the river Wye have often been painted, but the grandeur of the scene, looking from the heights above the junction of the two rivers (the Wye and the Severn), has seldom been so well depicted. This large landscape was painted entirely on the spot. This is Mr. Johnson's

No. 811.   *"The Wye and the Severn."*   C. E. JOHNSON.

51 × 84

"Le Dent du Géant."   E. T. COMPTON.

No. 297. *"Windsor under Snow."* V. P. YGLESIAS.

method, as distinct from many English artists we could name, who only make studies for their pictures in the open air. There is exceptionally fine quality of color in the rocky foreground on the left of this picture, which is worthy of a place in the National Gallery.

Mr. E. T. Compton takes us to the Chamouni district of Switzerland, with its glaciers and treacherous ice-fields. This carefully painted picture will scarcely have been noticed in the Academy, as it hung near the ceiling; but, as the sketch indicates, it is an elaborate and interesting transcript of nature that should not be overlooked.

No. 239. *"Rye."* V. P. YGLESIAS.

"Here flourish the flowers of the field,
Where once ships anchored."

No. 645. "*On the River*." G. Boyle.

The town of Rye, once a seaport, like Arundel in Sussex, the seat of the present Duke of Norfolk, stands high above the surrounding country, separated from the sea by miles of alluvial land covered with coarse grass and wild flowers. The interest in Mr. Yglesias's pictures is strong locally, for the artist at Windsor and at Rye has given us facts both in winter and spring.

Nothing could be brighter or more suggestive of early summer-time on English rivers,

31 × 66.

No. 582. "*May-time*." Basil Bradley.

No. 152. "*The Haunt of the Heron.*"

R. W. A. ROUSE.

No. 411. "*A Wintry Dirge.*"

ALFRED EAST.

when the white-thorn is in bloom, when the fresh green grows down to the water's edge, and the water-lilies are peeping their heads above the floating leaves, than Mr. Basil Bradley's picture of "*May-time*" (582). Such color and sunshine as are here depicted, Mr. Bradley, who is a skillful animal-painter, has given us often in water-colors at various exhibitions.

No. 865. "*The Ploughman homeward plods his Weary Way.*"

ALLEN C. SEALY.

No. 515. "*The Birthplace of the Brook.*"

Sir ARTHUR CLAY, Bart.

44 × 72.

No. 759.   *"Rievaulx Abbey."*   JOHN PEDDER.

39 × 60.

No. 745.   *"A Dappled Sky, a World of Meadows."*   F. WALTON.

37 × 60.

No. 264.   *"Across the Common."*   ADRIAN STOKES.

There is wind blowing through the trees in "*A Wintry Dirge*," by Alfred East (411); also in "*Across the Common*" (264), by Adrian Stokes. The character of some other land-scapes is indicated on these pages; Mr. Marmaduke Langdale's (1624) is well expressed, but Mr. Frank Walton, in 745, does injustice in his drawing to one of the best landscapes in the Academy. Sketches are also included here of works by G. Boyle, John Pedder in his little drawing, Sir Arthur Clay, Allen C. Sealy, T. Hope McLachlan, Frank Dillon, and R. W. A. Rouse.

24 × 36.

No. 1624. MARMADUKE A. LANGDALE.

Mr. W. L. Wyllie takes to the lower reaches of the Thames and Medway, crowded with barges and shipping at high water. He is one of the few young artists who have turned to account the busy aspects of the lower Thames, and shown us how steamers, steam-tugs, and even iron bridges, can be made picturesque. There is ample material here, especially near high water, when the great steamers are arriving at the port of London.

Another picture by Mr. W. L. Wyllie (1589), "*The Close of a Winter's Day*," shows the shattered hulk of an old "man-of-war," where a gang of convicts are being marched

No. 539. "*Heave away!*" (*Barges upward bound, shooting Rochester Bridge.*) W. L. WYLLIE.

14

No. 206. "*On Morecambe Sands.*"   T. Hope McLachlan.

"*The Pyramids of Egypt—Sunset.*" Frank Dillon.

No. 928. "*My Love has gone a-sailing.*" David Murray.

No. 1589. *"The Close of a Winter's Day."* W. L. WYLLIE.

through the snow from work—a strange subject, treated with considerable dexterity and power.

Mr. Peter Graham, R.A., paints mountains, sea, and mist, and sometimes heads of Scotch cattle on the hills. This year he has given us a striking and solemn landscape of *"Dawn"* among the mountains. Mr. Graham, like Mr. Colin Hunter, A. R. A. (whose *"Herring-Market at Sea"* is sketched on page v), is one of a company of Scotch landscape-painters of undoubted force and character. Mr. Graham and Mr. Hunter are representative of a class of Scotch painters who have earned the distinction of being denounced annually in the columns of the London "Athenæum," while the latter has lately been praised in an article by William Morris, poet and art-critic, a writer who has few good words for any member of the Academy. Mr. Colin Hunter's *"Herring-Market"* is a fine, suggestive

No. 27. *"Dawn."* PETER GRAHAM, R. A.

picture, rather coarsely painted, but composed with skill. Mr. Graham's work has the appearance of a direct transcript from nature. Like his beautiful "*Sea-Mist*," sketched below,
it is landscape portraiture seen under various atmospheric conditions.

As thorough in the analysis of atmospheric effects on sea and shore, but more finished
in detail, are the works of Mr. John Brett, A. R. A., who generally chooses sunny effects on
the English coast, where there is water of the purest blue, and where rocks are bathed in
sunshine. In "*MacLeod's Maidens*" the interest is much taken up in the resemblance to

No. 216.   "*Sea-Mist.*"   PETER GRAHAM, R. A.

human beings of the notorious rocks off the Isle of Skye, a resemblance which the artist has
made the most of, if not exaggerated. But we have no painter of calm blue sea to equal
Mr. Brett. He has also painted Granton Pier in a storm, but the painter of wind and high
seas is Mr. Henry Moore, who flits about the English Channel like the stormy petrel, delight-
ing in a gale; his wave-drawing is unsurpassed, and his studies of clouds are, as in old
Dutch pictures, an important part of the composition.

A mention of all the pictures of rivers, sea, and sea-coast, which crowded the Academy
walls this year, would fill a separate volume; we insert a few more sketches before passing
to the portraits. Many other landscapes will be found in the Grosvenor Gallery section
and in the water-colors.

Portrait-painting is not a branch of art which is especially interesting to illustrate by
sketches, but a few words must be devoted to it here, as the British school of portraiture

45 × 72.

No. 395. *"MacLeod's Maidens, Skye."* (*Natural Sculpture.*) J. Brett, A. R. A.

34 × 56.

No. 337. *"Calm Weather in Torbay."* Harry Colls.

30 × 54.

No. 1626. *"Off the Lizard, Penzance: Boats starting east for the Fishing."* Henry Moore.

is historically famous. Of the seven presidents of the English Royal Academy, Reynolds, West, Lawrence, Shee, Eastlake, Grant, and Leighton, four were professed portrait-painters, while all of them practiced the limner's art to an appreciable extent. But, in addition to these, there have been men like Kneller—the only artist who was ever made a baronet

No. 251. *"Mrs. William Huntington and Child."* JAMES SANT, R. A.

—Opie, Raeburn, Hoppner, Jackson, and Romney, all portrait-painters of a marked genius that would have distinguished them in any country and in any age. Some masters, like Holbein, Kneller—to whom we have referred—Vandyck, Lely, and others, although foreigners by birth, made England their home by adoption, and fostered and brought to maturity art tastes indigenous to the soil. The characteristics of British portraiture have ever remained—representation based upon truthfulness as a leading principle, no mere map of face or form, but that likeness which disclosed individuality and the character and dispo-

sition of the person represented. This class of portraiture, governed by good taste, has been the foundation
of our school of art in this branch; and, like portrait-
painting in general, it has furnished us with the best
kind of history of which the art of painting is capable.
Henry VIII, despotic and selfish as he certainly was,
was fortunately a man of learning, and, whether from
love of magnificence or other causes, greatly delighted
in gathering around him the most famous painters of
his time. To this monarch Englishmen must ever be
grateful for the introduction of Hans Holbein to England, and the life-work of Holbein is the best historical
essay in pictured presentments of all the eminent men
of his period it is possible to imagine. Succeeding
monarchs, like the unfortunate King Charles I, were
not sparing of their patronage of great artists, and par-

35 × 22.

No. 453. *"Miss Hardcastle."*

R. Lehmann.

ticularly of those whose craft was portraiture, so that, as a consequence, the history of our
country has been pretty faithfully brought down to the present day. Impressions conveyed
to the mind through the medium of sight, as in pictorial representation, are more powerful
than words, either written or spoken; and hence it may be that a fine portrait of Oliver
Cromwell, Martin Luther, or Drake, the great discoverer, at once arouses familiar associa-

46 × 72.

No. 851. *"The late Duke of Buccleuch, K. G."*

Knighton Warren.

tions connected with those remarkable men,
which serve, perhaps, more truly the purpose
of history than the best account ever written.
Thus, in portraiture we may have presented
to the mind the leading events of history,
such as the overthrow of a great monarchy
or the discovery of a new continent. But in
the late exhibition of the Royal Academy
there were few historic portraits; our great
artists are content with simple transcripts,
usually treated, it is true, with originality and
power. This is the case with the Academicians Millais, Watts, W. W. Ouless, and Frank
Holl, with the exception, indeed, that the last-
named master exhibits a noble whole-length

No. 139. *"Never mind!"*   FREDERICK MORGAN.

portrait of the Prince of Wales in his robes as Master of the Bench of the Honorable
Society of the Middle Temple.

Millais, Watts, Alma-Tadema, Holl, and Herkomer were well represented at the Grosvenor Gallery in portraiture, but Messrs. James Sant and Ouless are better known in the
Academy.   Mr. James Sant, R. A., who is portrait-painter in
ordinary to her Majesty the Queen, is, like his younger brother
Academician, Mr. W. W. Ouless, in taste, feeling, and artistic
training, essentially a portrait-painter.   This is not altogether the
case with Millais, Holl, and Watts, whose adoption of this
branch of art is comparatively recent, their reputations having
been made in historical, idealistic, and other subjects of a very
different class.   Mr. Sant has to a great extent monopolized the
field of female portraiture, his great compeers, Messrs. Ouless
and Holl, rarely venturing upon other than male likenesses.   In
our engraving of Mr. Sant's picture of *"Mrs. William Hunt-
ingdon and Child"* the special facility the artist has in at once
perceiving and seizing upon the more graceful traits of female
character, whether in childhood or in those of more mature
years, will readily be observed.   The natural ease and refinement
of this group are characteristic of all the master's work of this

No. 592.   *"Miss Nettie
Husley."*
Mrs. JOHN COLLIER.

YOU A CHRISTIAN
James Mason

class. There are younger painters rising up, such as Mr. John Collier and Mr. Wirgman, on whom the mantle may one day fall; but at the present moment the truth remains that portrait-painters of ladies in England are few and far between.

No. 750.   "*Watching the Effect.*"   S. SIDLEY.

No. 453, "*Miss Hardcastle,*" is, if a little conventional in treatment, a capital character study. Rudolph Lehmann, to whose powerful pencil we are indebted for some excellent portraits, has also in the galleries at Burlington House a life-like presentment of the eminent surgeon, Sir Spencer Wells, the President of the College of Surgeons in London.

Mr. Warren's portrait of "*The late Duke of Buccleuch*" pictures the duke, seated at full length in his library, in a (with him) characteristic and easy attitude. In preserving the like-

No. 136. *"Daughters of Colin Makins, M. P."*
JOHN COLLIER.

No. 1564. *"Geoff, Polly, Dolly, and Toto."*
FREDERICK BARNARD.

ness and Scotch type of face, the artist also has not forgotten the expression of thoughtful intelligence which characterized the original.

No. 139, *"Never mind,"* by Frederick Morgan, presents to us an image of childish innocence and beauty. One little tot, of but some five summers, has broken the toy she holds upon her lap, and her sister, of but very few years older, is playing the part of the good Samaritan as she caressingly whispers words of comfort to the little mourner. What grace there is in childhood, and charm in sympathy, the artist has here certainly found and expressed.

No. 592, *"Miss Nettie Huxley,"* by Mrs. John Collier, is a picture of a young lady standing facing the spectator. The artist, Mrs. Collier, is wife of Mr. John Collier, the well-known portrait-painter, who exhibits no less than four works in the present exhibition.

No. 83. *"Miss Fortescue"*
WEEDON GROSSMITH.

In No. 750, *"Watching the Effect,"* the artist, S. Sidley, gives a fancy title to what is evidently a portrait. A little girl in dark dress has planted herself upon a garden-seat, and there, with a dish of soap-suds and tobacco-pipe, is amusing herself blowing bubbles. She is not alone in her amusement, for her pet, a quaint little kitten, watches her young mistress's experiments with infinite curiosity and interest.

No. 136, May, Agatha, Veronica, and Audrey,

"*Daughters of Colin Makins, M. P.*," by John Collier, is an original group in spring costumes, with almond-blossoms and daffodils, primroses and wild flowers, on a polished floor; and No. 1564, "*Geoff, Folly, Dolly, and Toto,*" by Frederick Barnard, is a pretty group of children, a boy and his two sisters with their favorite dog.

No. 483, "*Miss Fortescue,*" by Weedon Grossmith, is a head study of the popular and pretty actress about whom there has recently been so much said with reference to an action for breach of promise.

No. 351. "*Rebellion on the Throne,*"   F. G. COTMAN.

No. 351, "*Rebellion on the Throne,*" by Frederick G. Cotman. The title here is but a play upon words; the throne in question merely being the raised platform upon which a portrait-painter places his sitter. The child, who serves as a model, is a pretty little girl,

24 × 18.

No. 655. "*Melody.*" G. H. BARRABLE.

whose waywardness is apparent, for around her are a guitar and other objects which have evidently been employed in the hopeless task of making her sitting for her portrait a less distasteful proceeding. With one shoe kicked off, and nursing her last bribe in the shape of a peacock's feather, she has now, however, by chance, thrown herself into the very posture for a successful picture, and of this the artist has not hesitated to avail himself.

Another picture, which may properly be described as of portrait class, is No. 655, "*Melody,*" by G. H. Barrable, a young lady performing on the violin, an instrument that only a recent fashion has deemed suitable for those of her sex. The instrument, however, admits of graceful posture in the performer, and is, perhaps, second to none when skilfully played upon.

No. 912, "*Philip Henry Gosse, Jr.,*" by Miss E. M. Osborn, is a whole-length portrait

31 × 15.

No. 712. "*Philip Henry Gosse, Jr.*"
E. M. OSBORN.

45 × 30.

No. 868. "*The Burgomaster's Daughter.*"
HUGH CARTER.

of a pretty little boy of some seven or eight summers; there is childish grace about the figure, and much innocent character in the bright, young face.

With the mention of No. 868, "*The Burgomaster's Daughter*," by Hugh Carter — a simple but extremely agreeable study of a young lady busy plying needle and thread — we will for the present return to other pictures.

No. 797. "*The Students at the British Museum.*" T. PECKITT.

No. 797, "*Students at the British Museum*," by T. Peckitt. Those studying art at the museum are, so to speak, free lances as compared with those working upon an organized system and under competent instruction at the Royal Academy, to which we shall immediately refer. But students not unfrequently make their work at the museum serve as a stepping-stone by which to obtain admission to the schools of the Academy; and it is needless to say that they at any rate have splendid models to copy from in the various antique busts, original statues, and other art treasures like the Elgin marbles. Mr. Peckitt's picture is at least illustrative, and gives a fair idea, both of the more isolated manner of work of the students, as well as of the archæological and other objects by which they are surrounded.

No. 106, "*The Life-School,*" by Florence Martin. The design pictures students at work drawing and painting from the live model, and the subject is peculiarly interesting, if only from the fact that it illustrates the working of one of the most important branches of free education in England. One of the leading objects of "the Royal Academy of Arts in London," founded by George III in 1769, as we learn from the memorial presented to the king asking his approval of such an academy, was "the establishment of a well-regulated school or Academy of Design for the use of students in the arts, while it was hoped that the funds to be derived from an annual exhibition of works of art by artists of merit would be sufficient to defray the expenses of the scheme." With the foundation of the Royal Academy came this all-important art-instruction. A "keeper" was appointed, who was also a member of the society, and to him was intrusted the general conduct and superintendence of the schools, while, in addition, other members of the Academy were annually appointed, who were called "visitors," and who were more directly concerned in teaching upon the occasions of the periodical visits they made to the schools. In addition to this, professors were appointed, who lectured annually on the various branches of art. And it perhaps may not be out of place to refer here incidentally to those discourses by the first president, Sir Joshua Reynolds, which, whether in regard to diction or the simple but noble expression of thoughtful ideas upon art, have ever since been regarded as a text-book, aiding the uncertain steps of the young, while they have added to the knowledge of those of more mature years. Such, in a few words, were the general principles upon which the scholastic system of our leading art was founded. As regards the details, it may, perhaps, hardly be necessary to say more here than that there were different schools — the antique, painting, and live-model schools — while the system by which admittance was obtained in the first instance to the privilege of studentship was by submission of a drawing by the candidate, which, if approved, entitled him to entrance as a probationer, when, if his first work was sustained by the merit of others

52 × 33

No. 106. "*The Life-School.*"

F. MARTIN.

executed within the walls of the Academy, he became a full student, and, according to the ability he displayed, could pass on to the higher and more important branches of study. In addition to this, rewards in the shape of gold and silver medals, and a "traveling student-ship," enabling the successful aspirant to study art abroad for a series of years, gave further substantial encouragement to those proving themselves worthy.

No. 63. *"Girl reading."* Mrs. A. Schenck.

Without entering upon the somewhat disputed point as to whether teaching which is not paid for is of value, we may add that the whole system of art-instruction, undertaken by the Royal Academy, is free of any cost or charge whatever.

The number of students admitted to the schools, for the first twelve years from the institution of the Academy in 1769, was three hundred and eighty-four, at a cost of no less than £10,826 17s. 6d. As compared with this, there are, at the present time, just upon four hundred students, while the cost amounts to between £5,000 and £6,000 per annum. Without attempting to specify, we may here mention the fact generally, that some of our most eminent artists followed out their early course of art-instruction in the schools of the Academy.

In the year 1860 the great principles of human progress and, no doubt, the influence of public opinion, produced a remarkable event in the history of the Academy schools, and female students were for the first time admitted.

There have only been two female Royal Academicians—Angelica Kauffman and Mary Moser, who were foundation members. There is a feeling against the election of women as members of the Academy, it being felt that in a large institution of this character many of the details, such as the arrangements for studying from the nude model, and some other matters, are not proper for the other sex. There is a prejudice that women art-students, like female doctors, barristers, and the deaconesses whom it is proposed should read the lessons in church, are really favored with more of the masculine mind than of that tender modesty with which one is so proud to associate the name of woman.

Thinking this brief sketch of the art educational system of our Royal Academy might prove not uninteresting, we will now return to the subject of the pictures.

No. 457. *"St. Peter denying Christ."* W. MOUAT LOUDAN.

No. 457. *"St. Peter denying Christ,"* by W. Mouat Loudan, is the work for which the young artist succeeded in obtaining the gold medal in the Academy schools. The recreant disciple who could so readily deny all knowledge of his Lord, sits upon a bench, looking the craven coward he was for the time being, while his accuser, a young girl, utters the words which may condemn him. The group is skillfully conceived, and the picture is executed in a low key of color, which is in sympathy with the tale of shame.

No. 1282, "*A Design for an Academy of Arts,*" by Edwin George Hardy. The artist is another of the successful Academy students, he having succeeded in gaining a gold medal

No. 1282. "*An Academy of Arts.*" EDWIN G. HARDY.
(Royal Academy Gold Medal and Traveling Studentship.)

and traveling studentship. He is among the class of architectural students, and his design is really one of very considerable merit and promise.

We hear, with much satisfaction, that, in the additions and alterations now making to the premises of the Royal Academy, extended space will be given to the architectural portion of the annual exhibitions.

A few words must be devoted to the water-colors in the Royal Academy. Aquarelle art has ever been popular in this country, for the labors of men like Turner, Girtin, David Cox, Dewint, and William Hunt, have served to establish work of this class in public estimation; and, at the present time, there are to be found not a few connoisseurs who restrict their collections wholly to examples of water-color art. We do not look to the Royal Academy Exhibition or the Grosvenor Gallery for the best specimens of the art, for,

28 × 41.

No. 1103. *"After Dinner."* (*Water-color.*) A. M. Rossi.

as a rule, members of the two great water-color societies, of whom we shall speak presently, restrict their attention to the periodical shows at their own institutions, with the result that only as an exception are the finest specimens to be found in the galleries at the Academy.

No. 936. *"Scraping an Acquaintance."* A. W. Strutt.

Still, the visitor to the water-color room at Burlington House will not fail to consider it rich in many clever drawings. No. 1103, "*After Dinner,*" by A. M. Rossi, is a good

No. 948. "*Gossip.*" J. H. HENSHALL.

example—a drawing brilliant and dashing in execution. The subject, four girls seated in the corner of a drawing-room, fairly illustrates a phase of English society.

No. 936, "*Scraping an Acquaintance,*" by Alfred W. Strutt, is a stable-man engaged in grooming a white horse at a stable-door. Forgiving the *double entendre* in the title of the work, this is a capital study of both the animals and human being. The noble dog, seated hard by, looks placidly content that his time for the cleansing process, to which the horse submits with but an ill-grace, has not arrived; the dog appears slightly out of scale.

No. 1156. *"A Fair Librarian."* Miss Edith Gourlie.

No. 948, *"Gossip,"* by J. Henry Henshall, pictures a couple of good dames enjoying to their hearts' content a chat by the way. One old lady, basket on her arm, is on her way to market, and the other is returning to her cottage with the two pails of water she has just placed upon the ground, while, with hands upon her hips, she relieves her mind of burning news.

No. 1156, *"A Fair Librarian,"* by Edith Gourlie, is a single-figure study of a tall—

No. 85. *"An English Home — Twilight."* HERBERT LYNDON.

No. 1014. *"Near Roby, Cheshire."* MATTHEW JARVIS.

No. 1155. *"Old Inn and Buildings at Hemel Hempstead."* W. J. MONTAIGNE.

No. 99. *"An Old English Inn."* HERBERT A. OLIVIER.
(Royal Academy Chadwick Prize, 1883.)

extremely tall—but graceful young lady standing in the library, reading the book held in one hand, while the other rests upon a feather brush. An arm-chair, two portfolios, and some library-steps, complete the picture.

No. 1234. "*An Old Manor-House.*" J. Langham.

No. 85, "*An English Home—Twilight,*" by Herbert Lyndon. A homestead buried in trees, with grassy fields and river seen under the influence of a light sky.

No. 1014, "*Near Raby, Cheshire,*" by Matthew Jarvis. Flat meadow scenery, with pool of water and trees.

In No. 1155, "*Old Inn and Buildings at Hemel Hempstead*," by W. J. Montaigne, the old roofs, the barn, the quaint-looking chimneys, and the peep of the village church, together form a study which is not without a certain picturesque charm suggestive of the quiet of of many a country town near London. But for a real old English inn of olden time, with carved exterior timbers, such as exist in Norfolk and Suffolk and near the old seaports of England, we must look next at No. 99, Mr. H. A. Olivier's drawing.

The motive of the design is one of those large, roomy, wayside inns, now rarely to be met with. As far as the idea of space gives comfort, these curious buildings were a success, but modern progress and the requirements of a more advanced civilization have tended to sweep away such old landmarks, their place being now gradually supplied by edifices more compact, convenient, and at the same time more sightly as regards the architecture. In this constantly recurring change the artist suffers as far as the picturesqueness of his subject is concerned; for, pictorially considered, the old stage-coach is but ill superseded by the locomotive or the tram-car; the ironclad is a sorry substitute for the grand-looking, old three-decker; and the smart, formal street rows of modern London call forth no artist enthusiasm as do the curious old building Mr. Olivier has placed before us. But human progress must be served, and, come what may, we must move forward. Not quite so early in the history of this country is the date of "*An Old Manor-House*," drawn by J. Langham (No. 1234), but it is a further illustration of our remarks. Many of the noble ancestral halls, of which this picture is a good example, exist in England more as curiosities, and because of their antiquity or from family or other associations, than from any recognized idea of comfort or other than the mere beauty of appearance. The necessity for semi-castellated buildings for purposes of defense has passed away, so that such edifices under a more advanced social system remain but as landmarks of a picturesque age.

It may, perhaps, be asserted, without much fear of contradiction, that the highest kind of representative art is that which best reproduces human form, and expresses the passions, sentiments, and mental characteristics of man. In that respect sculpture appears to stand pre-eminent, for, while the art of painting has wider aims and more extended resources, it lacks the simple dignity of an art which has for a leading motive the expression of perfect form, without the adventitious aid of coloring or other appeals to the senses. If, therefore, we may take the advance made in this, the highest of all arts, as in some sort an indication of progress in the people, it will have been noticed with satisfaction that the collection of sculpture this year at the Academy is better than in many previous seasons.

WALES.

T. B. KENNINGTON.

Among the works of the elder members of the Royal Academy we should mention first No. 1688, "*Egypt*," by H. H. Armstead, R. A.; a graceful, idealized female figure — statuette — typifying that ancient and remarkable country to which now for some time past the attention of European statesmen and financiers has been so strongly directed.

No. 1688. "*Egypt.*" H. H. Armstead, R. A.

No. 1700. "*The Water-Lily.*" T. Woolner, R. A.

No. 1700, "*The Water-Lily,*" by T. Woolner, R. A., represents a bathing nymph, who, before she entirely throws off her drapery, toys with her foot among the water-lilies, balancing her body in a position of ease, as she rests her weight upon her right hip. This, which is Mr. Woolner's only contribution, is a high-relief in bronze.

One of the most prominent and noteworthy works was No. 1856, "*The Mower,*" by Hamo Thornycroft, A. R. A., a comparatively young sculptor. A young hay-maker, wearing his straw hat, the upper part of his body bare, carries his shirt upon his arm, and with his scythe leisurely returns from his day's labors. The idea suggested is one of repose, this rustic figure being a fine example of Mr. Thornycroft's powers of modeling. There are two or three fine views of this statue of "*The Mower.*"

Mr. Thomas Brock, one of the newly elected Associates, sent a model of the marble bust of Longfellow in Westminster Abbey, and Mr. C. B. Birch the large statue of "*Lady Godiva*" (see page 133). Mr. Birch established for himself a reputation when he produced the colossal statues of Lieutenant Hamilton, killed in the Indian massacre, and "*The Last Call*," a bugler and his charger killed by the same shot; and this he has followed with his present masterly group of "*Lady Godiva*" and her steed, No. 1823.　The work, being tentative

No. 1856.　"*The Mower*."　HAMO THORNYCROFT, A. R. A.

"A mower, who, as the tiny swell of our boat passing heaved the river grass,
Stood with suspended scythe to see us pass."—MATTHEW ARNOLD, *Thyrsis*.

in character, is at present produced only in imitation bronze, but it is to be hoped the sculptor will be asked to execute it in the genuine metal, and that it may become national property.　Mr. Birch has represented the beautiful spouse of rough Earl Leofric standing beside her horse—a noble-looking animal. The pretty legend upon which the subject is founded may or may not be true, but certainly Mr. Birch's realization of the story could hardly be better; the figure of the self-sacrificing wife of the lord of Coventry being a most graceful conception, and the face particularly pure and lovely.

No. 1823. "*Lady Godiva.*" C. B. BIRCH, A. R. A.

". . . Anon she shook her head,
And showered the rippled ringlets to her knee;
Unclad herself in haste; adown the stair
Stole on; and, like a creeping sunbeam, slid
From pillar unto pillar, until she reached
The gateway; there she found her palfrey trapped
In purple, blazoned with armorial gold."

No. 1680, "*Linus,*" the personification of a dirge of lamentation, by E. Onslow Ford. The whole-length figure of this classic poet is here represented with right hand raised, while in the other he holds a torch thrust downward toward the ground. He is advancing with slow and solemn steps, repeating as he goes his words of grief and sorrow. It will be noticed in the reproduction how excellent is the swing of the figure and learned the modeling.

In No. 1684. "*Ruth and Naomi,*" the sculptor, J. Warrington Wood, seeks to realize in marble that most pathetic incident in which the widowed daughter-in-law elects to return

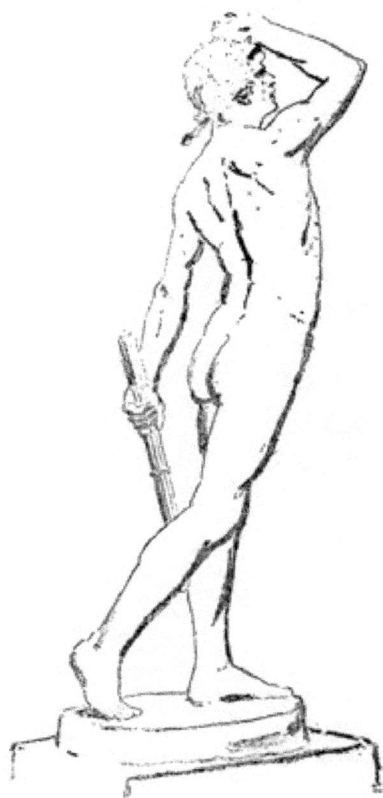

No. 1680. "*Linus.*" E. Onslow Ford.

with Naomi to her native place. Naomi has lost her husband Elimelech and both her sons, and now, bankrupt in everything save the love of one of her son's widows, she seeks to turn her weary and aged footsteps toward Bethlehem, whence she came. But Ruth's strong love will not be denied, and she sums up her determination when she employed that memorable phrase:

"Entreat me not to leave thee, or to return from following after thee."

The girl stands with her arms clasped lovingly round the aged woman's form, as she gives utterance to her tender appeal.

No. 1809, "*Ave, Cæsar! morituri te salutant,*" by George A. Lawson. This is one of the more important statues, a Retiarius who is standing with his head raised and thrown backward, while he holds aloft his trident in one hand, in the other being gathered the folds of his net. The figure is well balanced and good in line, the muscularity being of the order which suggests proportion without coarseness.

No. 1684. "*Ruth and Naomi.*"

J. WARRINGTON WOOD.

In the bronze statuette, No. 1746, "*Hercules,*" by G. Natorp, the celebrated hero and son of Jupiter is seen resting upon the brass club given him by Vulcan. The following lines suggest the motive of the design:

"Leaning dejected on his club of conquest,
As if he knew the worthlessness of those
For whom he had fought."

No. 1809. "*Ave, Cæsar! morituri te salutant.*"
G. A. LAWSON.

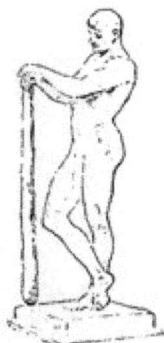

No. 1746. "*Hercules.*"
G. NATORP.

No. 1682. "*Bless me, even me also, O my Father,*" by E. Roscoe Mullins. The group here represented is very expressive. Esau, just returned from hunting, and robbed of his birthright by the deceit practiced upon his father by Jacob, has approached his aged and

No. 1682. "*Bless me, even me also, O my Father.*" E. R. MULLINS.

well-nigh sightless father, asking for the blessing he has a right to expect. But he has been forestalled, and, by words which can not be recalled, he has been given as a servant to his brother, upon whom also the richness of his father's blessing has fallen. Finding this to be the case, he cries to his father, with a loud and bitter cry, also for a blessing. The parent,

No. 1776. "*A Life-Size Sketch at the Zoo.*" G. SIMONDS.

while acknowledging the injustice of which by deceit he has been made guilty, endeavors to supplement his former words, which, however, he can not withdraw. The subject is very finely designed and rendered.

No. 1776, "*A Life-Size Sketch at the Zoo*," by George Simonds, is a noble model of a lion to be erected at Reading, near London, as a memorial to officers and men of the Sixty-sixth Berkshire Regiment who fell during the Afghan campaign, 1879–'80.

No. 1739. "*Kassasseen.*" A. M. CHAPLIN.
(Model for silver cup.)

No. 1740. "*A Study of Action.*" ARTHUR CLAY.

No. 1739. "*Kassasseen*," by Alice M. Chaplin. A spirited model of a Guardsman charging at the full speed of his horse, and who, as he charges, is engaged cutting down his enemy.

No. 1740, "*A Study of Action*," by Arthur Clay. A cow, which has been deprived of her calf, is wandering in distress. A small model, excellent in motion and action.

No. 1692. "*Miss Mary Anderson.*"
A. BRUCE JOY.

No. 1747. "*Fancy Head.*" (*Terra-cotta.*)
H. S. MONTALBA.

No. 1692, "*Miss Mary Anderson*," by A. Bruce Joy. The popular and beautiful actress, whose visit to England has been very like a triumphal procession, has here certainly been done justice to by the sculptor. It exhibits the quiet dignity, self-possession, and singular sweetness of expression that are characteristics of the face of the fair original, without any evidence of the self-consciousness which is too often present with such gifts.

A full-length portrait of "*The late Lord Frederick Cavendish*," No. 1678, also by the same sculptor, recalls the face and form of the unfortunate nobleman whose tragical fate

No. **1678**. "*The late Lord Frederick Cavendish.*" A. BRUCE JOY.
(Model of the statue to be erected at Barrow-in-Furness.)

will remain indelibly fixed in the memory in this country. Lord Cavendish has his right foot advanced, and holds his left hand upon his hip in a manner not unusual with him.

No. 1731, "*Regret*," by Frank Baden-Powell. A female head expressive of sorrow. The sculptor in this beautiful work ventures not unsuccessfully upon delineating a class of mental emotion which does not always tell its exact story in the human face. Direct physical pain, as in "*The Dying Gladiator*," or in the priest of the "*Laocoön*" group, is more readily reproduced than are the negative emotions of our nature. But Mr. Baden-Powell has fear-

lessly ventured into this more subtile and difficult region of art, and he may be congratulated upon the result. Almost the last of the sculptors to whom we can draw attention this
year is Miss H. S. Montalba, one of a very gifted family, no less than five members of
which contributed to the present exhibition. Miss H. S. Montalba, the sculptor, is seen to
advantage in No. 1747, the pretty study in terra-cotta of a child. With little more scope
in such a subject than is afforded by an ordinary portrait-bust, Miss Montalba has managed

No. 1731. *"Regret."* F. BADEN-POWELL.

to invest the face with a character of childish beauty that is peculiarly charming. It is not
often that the artistic faculty is apparent in so many members of a family as it is in that
of the Montalbas. The spontaneous character and grace of style of this lady's work are
very closely allied to genius.

We select from the portrait-busts (not, as a rule, a very interesting department of any
exhibition) the presentment of one whose name and features are very familiar in London;
one whose interest in all art matters, and especially in international exhibitions, is well

known. "*Sir Philip Cunliffe Owen, K. C. M. G., etc.*," the head of the South Kensington
Museum, is a skilled administrator. He is especially interested in the dissemination of the
knowledge of English art in America at the present time; and, it is well known, is now
organizing an exhibition of American productions at South Kensington for 1886. The
young sculptor, Mr. R. A. Ledward, has accomplished a successful work, and has been
especially fortunate in his subject.

Life-size.

No. 1770. "*Sir Philip Cunliffe Owen, K. C. M. G., etc.*" (*Bust, terra-cotta.*) R. A. LEDWARD.

THE GROSVENOR GALLERY.

THE first exhibition of the Grosvenor Gallery was held on the 1st of May, 1877, and contained two hundred and nine works by living artists, the prominent exhibitor being Mr. E. Burne-Jones, who sent the six beautiful decorative panels entitled "*The Days of Creation*," now in possession of Mr. W. Graham; also "*Venus's Mirror*" and "*The Beguiling of Merlin*." In that year, also, Mr. G. F. Watts, R. A., sent his well-known picture of "*Love and Death*," and other prominent exhibitors were Sir Francis Grant, Sir Frederick Leighton, J. G. Millais, L. Alma-Tadema, Holman Hunt, W. B. Richmond, R. Spencer Stanhope, Walter Crane, J. M. Whistler, Professor Legros, and Richard Doyle.

Since that time there have been seven summer exhibitions, in which the predominant note has been a style of art in which the works of the Italian masters had more influence than Wilkie or Gainsborough.

The exhibition of 1884, although more miscellaneous in character than formerly, and containing some of the finest portraits of the year, is still presided over, so to speak, by the work of Mr. Burne-Jones. Never since the exhibition of "*The Wheel of Fortune*," of "*The Days of Creation*," and of "*The Four Seasons*," has so great an impression been made in the artistic world by any painting as by "*King Cophetua and the Beggar-Maid*,"

29 × 21.

No. 8. "*Portrait of Signor G. B. Amendola.*"
L. ALMA-TADEMA, R. A.

which hang in the place of honor in the large gallery. It may give the best idea of this picture and of the estimation in which it was held to give an extract from a criticism which appeared in the London "Times" on the day of the opening of the gallery:

"We are only echoing the opinion which is all but universal among those, whether artists or not, who have seen the picture, when we say that 'King Cophetua and the Beggar Maid' is not only the finest work that Mr. Burne-Jones has ever painted, but that it is one of the finest pictures ever painted by an Englishman. On an upright canvas, some nine feet high, the artist has represented two principal and two secondary figures—the king, the beggar-bride, and two chorister-boys who are making music in the gallery above. The groundwork of the picture consists of a curious throne, forming a kind of alcove in the palace, with steps and seats and columns in shining, beaten brass. The maiden is seated on the purple cushion, and on the step at her feet is the king, the jeweled iron crown in his hands, and his face fixed on hers with an expression of adoring love and wonder. She sits half-dismayed and half-content, shrinking from the greatness of this new and unknown fortune, yet ready to face it, as some saint might face the Beatific Vision, in the strength of her maiden purity. She is thin, as one should be who has fared poorly all her days; her shoulders and arms are somewhat drawn; even her beautiful face is a little wan with fasting. She wears a single garment of some gray, felt-like substance, falling close over her knees, and bound chastely across her breast and shoulders. Her feet are timorously drawn under her; with her hands she presses for support upon the throne. Cophetua sits below, glorious and radiant in all the colors that king may wear or painter imagine, in steel armor, plate, and chain, with robe of many tints thrown over him; the crown which he holds is resplendent with jewels, and the brass at his feet and all around him is bright and gleaming. His form and the expression of his face are singularly noble; he is, in fact, every inch a man, a true king and knight, before whose arm and knee many an enemy has gone down."

The artist has gone for his theme to an old legend of no very wide notoriety till Tennyson brought it back to the knowledge of mankind, and thus far, perhaps, it must be admitted, he has chosen less worthily than when he painted his allegory of "*The Wheel of Fortune*" or his "*Days of Creation*." Yet, on the other hand, it is a story which almost explains itself, and even those who never heard of King Cophetua will understand that the picture marks a phase of the never-ending history of beauty triumphing over strength.

The great interest attaching to this picture, apart from its general design and rich qualities of color, is in the principal figure. "Mr. Burne-Jones has been commonly charged with 'inability to paint a hero,' but Cophetua is a hero," says the "Times"; and, as to his beggar-bride, "seldom has the lovely type, of which this painter has given us so many examples, been rendered with so much tenderness, dignity, and beauty as here." From the last sentence we may gather the fact that the beggar-maid is painted in Mr. Burne-Jones's well-known manner, and those who have seen his idealized pictures of women in England (or in America, where there are several), and know his color, will get very closely to the type; but his King Cophetua is altogether a new departure, more vigorous and original than anything yet seen from his hand.

Other critics contended that, great as is the picture, "the stickler for archæological accuracy may question the architecture and ornaments, the dress of the two pages in the gallery, and the armor of the king; and contend that these are hardly in accordance one with the other." But opinions coincided that "on the sentiment of the story he had the firmest grasp." "The monarch," one writes, "is undeniably enamored of the maiden in his presence, and hers is just as surely, as Tennyson puts it, 'a lovesome mien,' and her wan beauty and delicate, fanciful grace pierce through her poor attire

"'As shines the moon in clouded skies'"

At this point the feebleness of mere words to describe any picture is so manifest that in spite of the natural wish of the painter that no engraving should be made of a picture depending so much upon color and the artist's own handling for its ex-  pression, we insert a memory-note, or map of the principal lines. With this key to the composition, and the statement that the canvas is nine feet eight inches by four feet five, we must pass on to pictures by other artists, not omitting to mention that a very decorative and harmonious study in green, entitled "*A Wood-Nymph*," a single figure in green dress in the branches of a tree, also hung in the large gallery, by E. Burne-Jones.

Among the followers of Mr. Burne-Jones, or at least those who work in a similar spirit, we should mention Sir Coutts Lindsay, Mr. R. Spencer Stanhope, Mr. J. M. Strudwick, Miss Pickering, and Mr. Walter Crane. Mr. Stanhope's picture of "*Patience on a Monument*" is a labored work, marked by considerable knowledge and refinement; the draperies are red and blue, dark brown and green, almost as simple in scheme of color as an early Venetian fresco. In the distance there is an old-fashioned garden with statues, which are not seen in the sketch.

Mr. Walter Crane, whose decorative work is well known both in England and America, is a poet as well as a painter. "*The Bridge of Life*" is a picture teeming with incident and suggestion. So complete is it as a poem of life, "from the cradle to the grave," that we have thought it better to print the artist's own description of his work. Few painters in these days bestow more thought or invention on their subjects than Mr. Walter Crane:

"What is life? A bridge that ever
Bears a throng across a river;
There the Taker, here the Giver.

"What is life? In its beginning,
From the staff see Clotho spinning
Golden thread and worth the winning.

49 × 43

No. 211.   *"Patience on a Monument, smiling at Grief."*   R. SPENCER STANHOPE.

"Like patience on a monument,
Smiling at grief."—*Twelfth Night.*

"Life with life, fate-woven ever,
Life the web and love the weaver,
Atropos at last doth sever.

"What is life to grief complaining?
Fortune, Fame, and Love disdaining,
Hope, perchance, alone remaining.

"This design is figurative of human life in its various phases from the cradle to the grave. Life, in the collective sense—life in continuity—is expressed, firstly, by the marble bridge spanning the stream of time, veined and shot with various dyes and stains; viewed as a compact and interdependent whole, rising to its key-stone, with its stairs and stages, from the water's edge, where its foundings are hidden. Next life, as in its individual sense —the course of humanity—may be traced. Here the young mother receives her first-born from the arm of the Genius of Life. The father, with one foot raised, as if about to ascend the stair, and bearing the water-jar, the loaves and fishes—figuring the means for the sup-

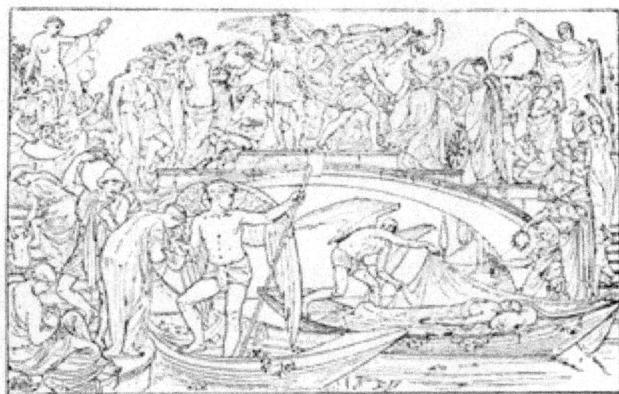

No. 206. *"The Bridge of Life."* WALTER CRANE.

port of life—turns to look at his child. Upon the steps a mother suckles her child, and above is teaching the infant to walk. As a boy he is taught by an old man from a scroll. Beyond rises the figure of Clotho, spinning—the Fate presiding over the beginnings of life, as living and human, but standing apart as a statue, a passionless but half-pitying spectator. Below her a girl and boy are playing, the boy blowing bubbles, which rise in the air and are lost. Next come a pair of lovers, or a bride and bridegroom, as she is crowned with myrtle; on the next step above, the little god Love, held aloft on the shoulder of one of the Graces, showers roses upon them. A satyr, or we may call him Pan—as representing the animal impulses—holding his pipes, clings to the man in his prime, who stands above the key-stone of the bridge, half turning, with a cup of glass in his hand, which the nymphs of Venus fill with wine, or make fragrant with roses. Behind him a winged genius—Fame, or Ambition—holds a wreath above his head and blows a trumpet; which things indicate

24 × 36.

No. 38. "*Aphrodite.*" PHILIP H. CALDERON.

"Fresh as the foam."

that in life's prime, when 'all thoughts, all passions, all delights' are in full stream, man is stimulated by ambition to win other prizes, and reluctantly turns from the pleasures of

28 × 36.

No. 222. "*By the Tideless, Dolorous, Midland Sea.*" MRS. JOHN COLLIER.

youth. At his side a woman halts and pensively gazes downward, seeing the corse on the boat passing beneath the bridge, like those who, in life's mid-career, are crossed by the

AN UGLY CUSTOMER.

J. R. REID.

shadow of death. In front of her a man with a
winged helmet eagerly presses forward, and, grasping
by one hand the empty hand of Fortune, stretches
the other to reach the bag of gold she holds aloft,
and illustrates the well-known dictum concerning
Dame Fortune. Another aspirant has fallen in the
pursuit, and vainly stretches his hand for the unat-
tainable prize. A companion figure of Fortune turns
her wheel; and lower down a woman half sadly and
regretfully gazes backward—a Lot's wife sighing for
the pleasures left behind and youth gone by—while
her companion stoops beneath the weight of a globe.
Thus doth man win fame, and the whole world, per-

No. 97. *"Once more."* W. E. F. Britten.

chance—he exchanges the glittering bubbles and dreams of his youth for solid earth, or
gold, or power, and has to bear the burden of it. A woman below him, with bowed head,
figures the despair of life—the shadow of success, the bane of wealth, the Nemesis of existence. An old man, leaning on his staff and on the shoulder of a youth, slowly descends
the steps of the bridge—age that knows his end is near, but is able calmly to meet it—
while the careless youth holds life like an apple to his lips. Behind these a figure of

No. 28. *"The Bath."* J. R. Weguelin.

No. 24. *"Soft Persuasion."* W. H. Bartlett.

Lachesis holds up a veil she has woven—the web of life, wrought with the memory of nights and days, with thought and action, with grief or delight, wherewith all life is clothed.

"Lower down on the steps Hope holds a lamp as she looks back on the stream of humanity, while Love, frighted at the figure of Death, clings to her side. Beneath these, again, a child has let fall a vessel of glass—'the false and fragile glass'—which lies broken upon the marble stair. He holds by the cloak of a woman bowed in grief, who is about to place a wreath upon the bier as the boat with its dark freight passes, and Atropos,

No. 85. *"The Farmer's Daughter."* W. Q. Orchardson, R. A.

kneeling at her side, with her shears snaps the thin golden thread which, from the infant in the arm of Life, can be traced all through the design till it is coiled at last in the hand of Death as he draws the pall over his last victim, and his barge, hung with garlands of poppies, glides on its silent way."

In a different spirit from the foregoing, a good deal later than the Renaissance, almost, it might be said, in the style of modern French art, is the "*Aphrodite*," by P. H. Calderon, which hung in the center of the great room. There is a peculiar dash and a brilliancy, apart from fine modeling, about this picture; in quality of color it might have been painted by Bouguereau, but there is more spontaneity here. It is difficult to picture to the mind, without color, the brightness of the blue sea, crested with foam, the sweep of the sea-gulls on the wind, the fair locks of "*Aphrodite*," and the beautiful form on the waves. As a design it is vigorous and striking, and is, to a certain extent, a new departure for this artist. The critics asked the question, "Where, with such successes as this picture, and the small study of a girl bathing of last year, is this artist to stop?" "Will he, as a member of the Academy, go further in the study of the nude, and place his pictures on the walls at Burlington House, where such subjects are seldom exhibited?"

Somewhat similar in aim, but quieter, more tentative, less sure of success, and, as a consequence, perhaps, more refined, is the delicate and original study of two figures on the shore of the Mediterranean Sea, by Mrs. John Collier, of whose work we have spoken on page 116. This picture is low in tone, with a pearly gray light over the sea and sand-hills, a curious contrast in treatment to Mr. Calderon's.

Two young artists may be mentioned together on this page. Mr. W. E. F. Britten has already made himself a name as a draughtsman of the figure, and has executed some fine decorative studies of boys and dolphins. He is at present engaged on some designs for the Earl of Leconsfield's house in London in conjunction with the architect, Mr. G. Aitchison, A.R.A. Mr. Britten's "*Flight of Helen*," a large picture, one of a series painted for Wyfold Court for the late Edward Hermon, M.P., was exhibited in the Grosvenor Gallery in 1881. His little picture in the Grosvenor Gallery (No. 97) is a study of color, the background, deep-blue sea melting into gray green on the wet sand.

No. 214. "*Far from the Madding Crowd.*"

R. W. MACBETH, A.R.A.

Mr. Bartlett has risen rapidly to the front as a painter of sea-coast scenes in various places. In 1881 he sent a study from the west coast of Ireland; last year, "*Bathing and Crab-catching on the Lagoons*" at Venice.

Mr. Weguelin is an experienced painter of small classic subjects, many of which have been seen in this gallery. Mr. Weguelin, Mr. Britten, and Mr. Bartlett are among the artists who owe much to the directors of the Grosvenor Gallery for the early recognition of their works.

No pleasanter specimen of Mr. Orchardson's art has been seen of late than his picture of "*The Farmer's Daughter*," an unimportant subject, calling for no great effort on the part of the painter, but exhibiting his skill and refinement of color—a scheme of yellow, brown, and gray; the girl in pink and white dress. But the statuesque little maiden, holding a pigeon on her wrist, is quite as mannered and characteristic of the artist as is Mr. R. W. Macbeth's fashionable lady in a high-crowned hat and feather in "*Far from the*

No. 87. "'*Twixt Day and Night.*" W. J. HENNESSY.

Madding Crowd," which the artist has sketched for us. The latter is bright and sunny to a degree, but, like Mr. Orchardson's, a picture more of color than of sentiment. There is a suggestive air of retrospection in the attitude of the lady, but the interest is attracted mainly to the dashing painting of costume and accessories. Mr. Macbeth was seen to best advantage in the Royal Academy.

There is sentiment and also truth to nature in Mr. W. J. Hennessy's landscape, "'*Twixt Day and Night*," with the Normandy peasants, old and young, passing through an orchard under the silver light of a summer moon. The figures are the strong point in the picture. All is harmonious and quiet, not to say prosaic, but the interest is great from an artistic point of view. Mr. Hennessy has drawn the figures separately and in the landscape, to give a better idea of the picture.

No. 121. "*Caller Herrin'*." David Carr.

"Wives and mithers maist despairin'
Ca' them lives o' men."

No. 151. "*Golden Hours.*"
J. P. Jacomb-Hood.

Mr. David Carr, the painter of "*La Force*" in 1883, is resting on his laurels. This year his subject is one of the heroines of Kingsley's poem, "*Caller Herrin'*," a somewhat unusual type of fisherwoman, as we are apt to picture them, but one that may be true to life, nevertheless.

Mr. Jacomb-Hood, like Mr. David Carr, has painted scenes from the history of the French Revolution; this year to the Grosvenor Gallery he sent "*Golden Hours*" (151), a graceful subject, well drawn and good in color.

Nos. 258, 14.   "*At the Fountain.*"   HAYNES WILLIAMS.

Mr. E. A. Waterlow sent a picture entitled "*A Saunter through the Fields*" — a rustic maiden walking through meadows, bright with poppies and white and yellow flowers; also

No. 93.   "*A Love 'Sett'*"   E. H. FAHEY.

"*The Shepherd's Return*," the pretty pastoral sketched on page 164. Here we want color to aid description; the freshness and airy effect of these landscapes are typical of much healthy English work. Mr. Haynes Williams's two pictures sketched above, if somewhat conventional in treatment, are thoroughly well painted. One of these subjects we have also reproduced as a photo-plate. This artist had also a small and interesting study of a table and chairs, tapestried wall and polished floor, in a used apartment at Fontainebleau. Apart from the skillful painting of textures, the artist managed to endow the furniture with quite a living interest, suggestive of former occupants and their history.

The pictures by Mr. E. H. Fahey, Mr. Edgar Barclay, Mr. Smallfield, and Mr. Arthur Lemon

No. 53. "*A Highwayman.*" ARTHUR LEMON.

No. 46. "*Rescued Fruit: A Flood at Athelney.*" EDGAR BARCLAY.

No. 245. "*King Log and King Stork.*" F. SMALLFIELD.

No. 35. *"The Rival Grandfathers."*   J. R. REID.

this year call for no special remarks. The feeling of landscape is strong in Mr. Barclay and Mr. Lemon. The latter has a good eye for color: the blue of the highwayman's coat is well balanced against the low-toned trees; the action is good, and the story well suggested.

The young Scotch artist, Mr. J. R. Reid, whose work we have already seen in the Academy, was well represented in the Grosvenor Gallery with his *"Rival Grandfathers,"* a picture which, had it been a little less coarsely painted and a little less uniform in its tone of blue, would have made the reputation of many an older painter. Nothing in the gallery was better than the drawing of the young fisher-girl, or more natural than the attitudes of the old men and child. A little more delicacy and sense of harmony in color seem to be the need of many young Scotch painters, such as Mr. David Murray, whose landscape hung near the foregoing.

No. 7. *"October."*   Miss FLORA M. REID.

"All is safely gathered in
Ere the winter storms begin."

No. 334. *"Favorites."*   (*Water-color.*)
Miss LIZZIE REID.

No. 185. "*The Song of the Sea-Birds.*"
W. Hughes.

No. 96. "*A Descent upon Italy.*"
Sydney P. Hall.

The sisters of Mr. John Reid were also exhibitors this year, one in oils and one in water-colors. The figure of the man in Miss Flora Reid's "*October*" is excellent.

Thoroughly decorative in spirit and design is the large silver panel by Mr. W. Hughes, which occupies a large space at the end of the East Gallery, over Mr. Richmond's portrait of "*May*" and Mr. North's landscape. These harmonies have all been considered in the hanging of the pictures in the Grosvenor Gallery.

No. 173. "'*One Good Turn deserves another.*'" J. Emms.

The motive of Mr. S. P. Hall's "*Descent upon Italy*" is best described in Plutarch's "Life of Caius Marcius." Speaking of the early wars of the inhabitants of the mountains, he writes: "They held their enemies in such contempt, and came on with so much inso-

No. 217.   "*Funeral of Thomas Carlyle, at Ecclefechan.*"   ROBERT W. ALLAN.

lence that, rather to show their strength and courage than out of any necessity, they exposed themselves naked to the showers of snow; and, having pushed through the ice and deep drifts of snow to the tops of the mountains, they put their broad shields under them, and so slid down in spite of broken rocks and vast slippery descents."

Mr. Emms and Mr. Beadle are two of the many young artists which this gallery has brought to the front, but whose pictures need no special description. More serious in motive is a sympathetically painted picture by a young Scotch artist, which was unfortunately placed in the gallery. "I made up my mind," Mr. Allan writes, "that Ecclefechan, the burial-place of Carlyle's own family, would be the place selected for the solemn ceremony; so I made a special journey, and arrived just in time to make notes of the place. No one was present at the funeral save his own kindred and the poor people of his native village, as everything had been kept secret."

No. 19.   "*Thro' Elizabeth, you must not leave us.*"
MRS. ALMA-TADEMA.

The funeral-procession of Thomas Carlyle is seen approaching along the snow-covered street, presently to turn into the gateway of the graveyard on the right of the picture. All was dark and drear; a leaden sky shrouding the muffled figures of the villagers waiting by the entrance in the wall; the "square, uncomely kirk," the snow-covered street, all ending in gloom, suiting well the temper of the departed.

Two little pictures, quiet in color and very carefully painted, No. 19, are by Mrs. Alma-Tadema; the one sketched is taken from the story of "The Burgomaster's Daughter."

On the walls of the Grosvenor Gallery, covered but a few months ago with the works of Sir Joshua Reynolds, some of our greatest living portrait-painters exhibited last season.

40 × 29.

No. 106. *"Portrait of the Marquis of Lorne."* J. E. MILLAIS, R. A.

It may be that in the comparative quiet of the Grosvenor Gallery, with less crowding and more care bestowed upon the juxtaposition of pictures, the Royal Academician finds a better place for the display of his pictures than at Burlington House. Certain it is that the spring exhibitions at the Grosvenor Gallery give the best idea of the style and quality of contemporary English portraiture. Three years ago there was a memorable collection of the works of G. F. Watts; and later, of those of L. Alma-Tadema. Last year there was a fine portrait of a boy, by E. Burne-Jones, in fifteenth-century manner; and occasionally Mr. Holman Hunt sends a portrait. This year, between the great exhibitions of the Reynoldses and the Gainsboroughs, we have had portraits by Millais, L. Alma-Tadema, Watts, Richmond, Holl, Herkomer, and many others.

The "*Portrait of the Marquis of Lorne*," by J. E. Millais, R.A., presented by the painter to the National Gallery of Canada, which hung at the end of the large room, is, as the sketch indicates, an extremely life-like presentment of the late Governor-General of the Dominion, and an excellent example of the artist's style. Two interesting portraits by the

90 × 33

No. 113.   "*Portrait of Miss Mary Anderson.*"   C. E. HALLÉ.

same hand, one of Miss Nina Lehmann as a child in 1868, in white dress seated on a green earthenware garden-seat, and another, of the same sitter, in white dress with golden background, as Lady Campbell, married in 1884, showed Millais at his best, and afforded opportunity for the comparison of his later and earlier methods of work. The "*Portrait of the Marquis of Lorne*," full of breadth and vigor, is rather sketchy; but here the requirements of portraiture have been more considered, and the details are put in with wonderful certainty and precision. Such portraits as these might well hang side by side with the older masters of the English school.

The portraits, by G. F. Watts, of Lord Salisbury and Lord Lytton, are characteristic of another and altogether different style, more subtile if less powerful than the foregoing, depicting the inner life rather than the outward characteristics of the man. It is said with much truth of Watts, that you must know the requirements of good portraiture, and the *character of the sitter*, to appreciate his work.

But nothing in the portraiture of the year has probably exceeded in power and unflinching realism the work of L. Alma-Tadema. In the Grosvenor Gallery there were three por-

59 × 32.

No. 31. *"Homeward."* RUDOLF LEHMANN.

traits by him, two of his friends, "*Signor G. B. Amendola*," sketched at the head of this section, the well-known sculptor working at a little silver statuette of Mrs. Alma-Tadema, and "*Herr Lowenstam.*" The third portrait, of "*Miss Lewis*," a young lady with jet-black hair, seated in white dress, is a technical triumph, the most powerful and realistic portrait in the room. But, in the details in the two first-named portraits, in the painting, for instance, of the head in the mirror, and of the surface of the copper-plate at which Herr Lowenstam is at work, and the green acid in the glass, Mr. Tadema is at his best, every detail adding character to the portraits.

No. 103. *"The Little Bookworm."*
Val. C. Prinsep, A.R.A.
36 × 27.

The graceful portrait of *"Miss Mary Anderson,"* by C. E. Hallé, which occupied one of the places of honor in the large room, has especial interest at present in England. She stands in easy attitude, in a light dress, with a copy of "Romeo and Juliet" in her hand—the play she was studying when her portrait was taken. Mr. Hallé has been very successful in several portraits of ladies, notably one of the wife of E. J. Poynter, R.A. At the time of writing it was not settled whether the portrait of *"Miss Anderson"* is to be engraved, but the handling and balance of light and shade would probably reproduce well.

Among the most prominent portrait-painters who exhibit in the Grosvenor Gallery we should have mentioned W. B. Richmond. His portraits of the two *"Miss Mirlees,"* nearly life-size—one seated, one standing, in green velvet dress and hat—had great distinction; and another, of a fair young girl, entitled *"May"* (No. 184), seated at a piano-forte in light-brown dress (recalling the *"St. Cecilia"* of Sir Joshua Reynolds, lately seen at Burlington House), is most delicately and harmoniously painted, showing this comparatively young artist's powers to great advantage.

40 × 50.
No. 86. *"Portrait of Mrs. Duff."* John Collier.

Near Mr. Richmond's works, and on either side of the great picture of "*King Cophetua*," were the portraits by F. Holl, R. A., Hubert Herkomer, A. R. A., and Rudolph Lehmann. These, especially the "*Lord Houghton*," by Lehmann, suffered in color from juxtaposition with Mr. Burne-Jones's picture. The portrait of "*Lord Brabourne*," by Herkomer, is a powerful likeness, and there were others by him in the gallery; but, altogether, the portraits of ladies and children may be said to have been the successes at the Grosvenor Gallery; including the "*Queen of the May*," by Herbert Schmalz, "*The Little Bookworm*,"

No. 197. "*Portrait of Madame Bodichon*."

Miss E. M. Osborne.

by Val C. Prinsep, and the works of James Sant, R. A., John Collier, and James Whistler.

The work of five ladies, portrait-painters, regular contributors to the exhibitions at the Grosvenor Gallery, may be mentioned together—Miss Osborne, Mrs. Jopling, Mrs. Merritt, Mrs. John Collier, and Mrs. H. M. Paget. Miss Osborne, whose well-known picture of "*The Governess*," in possession of the Queen, has been engraved and distributed into thousands of English homes, sent a life-size portrait of "*Madame Bodichon*," the wife of Dr. Eugène Bodichon, of Algiers. Madame Bodichon, herself a landscape-artist of considerable repute, is best known in England by her philanthropic work in connection with the education of women, and as one of the founders of Girton College at Cambridge. Miss Osborne depicts her friend at work in her country home at Hastings, in Sussex.

Mrs. Anna Lea Merritt, of Philadelphia, in her new studio, "The Cottage," Tite Street, Chelsea, surrounded by a little colony of artists (among them J. M. Whistler, Frank Miles, Frank Dicey, and Mr. and Mrs. John Collier), is busily engaged on portraits, among them one, finished but not yet

No. 160. "*Portrait of Mrs. F. E. Colman*."

Mrs. A. L. Merritt.

No. 112. *"Brunetta e Biondina."*
Mrs. H. M. Paget.

exhibited, of *"Mrs. Stirling,"* and *"Miss Ellen Terry"* in "Romeo and Juliet." Mrs. Merritt had the courage last year to send a life-size nearly nude figure of *"Camilla"* to the Academy, and this year had a picture (sketched on page 45) of the fair maiden and the knight in armor in *"La Belle Dame sans Merci"*—occupying a very large space on the Academy walls. The vigorous character of this artist's work, both in design and draughtsmanship, and the rapidly increasing quality of her *technique*, are generally admitted in London.

Mrs. H. M. Paget, living in Bedford Park, the so-called æsthetic village at Chiswick, near London, paints in the same studio with her husband, who exhibited this year at the Academy. The children in red and blue frocks, *"Brunetta e Biondina,"* painted by Mrs. Paget, are boldly and at the same time decoratively treated in brilliant colors, well harmonized.

Among the portrait-painters we should not omit to mention Mr. Felix Moscheles, whose portraits of himself and his wife in the Grosvenor Gallery are presented on this page. Mr.

No. 176. *"Mrs. F. Moscheles."*
F. Moscheles.

No. 183. *"Portrait of the Artist."*
F. Moscheles.

GOING TO THE FOUNTAIN.
Haynes Williams

Moscheles, the son of the well-known composer, is himself a musician, and in the London season his studio is crowded with musical celebrities as well as artists. When on a recent visit to New York, where he had a studio at the Park Avenue Hotel, Mr. Moscheles made the experiment of giving a practical lesson in portrait-painting, and illustrating his remarks by painting a portrait before an audience of about fifty persons. Those who were near enough, both to hear and to see Mr. Moscheles at work, gained a certain amount of knowledge of the methods and *technique* of the art; but it is open to question whether, excepting in art-schools, such teaching can be of much practical benefit. Mr. Moscheles is skillful in the art of *sketching* in a portrait in oils in an hour and a half, and has much to say that is of interest on the subject, but of the requirements of portraiture, and of the serious and arduous nature of the work, these sketch-lectures give little idea; and it is possible that a non-critical audience, attracted by such a *tour de force* as a life-size head growing upon the canvas before their eyes in less than two hours, may go away with the idea that portrait-painting is a rather overrated and overpaid profession. But Mr. Moscheles is serious in his art, and in his object of giving information to students by the eye as well as by the ear. The portraits of himself and Mrs. Moscheles are two out of many lately painted by this artist.

No. 257. *"Dulcie, Daughter of Philip Waterlow, Esq."*

WEEDON GROSSMITH.

Other portrait-painters, exhibitors in the Grosvenor Gallery in 1884, whose sketches appear on these pages, were Mr. Edward Hughes, Mr. Herbert Schmalz, Mr. Julian Story, and Mr. Weedon Grossmith.

The landscapes in the Grosvenor Gallery are seen to so much better advantage than in the Academy that critics may be apt to attach too much relative importance to them. But, just as certain figure-subjects, which we have admired here, would have been crowded out of sight in the great throng at Burlington House, so there are certain landscapes which it would have been impossible to appreciate or examine in the Academy. Among these we should mention first the work of Mr. J. W. North. *"Our Hedges and Ditches,"* by this artist, is an elaborate study of the undergrowth of early spring, a tangle of branches and blossoms, with innumerable varieties of twig and flower; a delicate net-work of Nature's weaving put on canvas with a loving hand. Such painting we seldom see attempted in oils; and the composition of it can not, as Mr. North says himself, be indicated in any sketch in black-and-white. But, unpretending as the subject is—the only human interest being in one or two girls gathering the last winter's sticks, painted on a very small scale—we are taken to it again and again as a rare bit of nature.

Much more obvious, both in motive and in handling, and as strong a contrast as we could find easily in one gallery, is the work of Miss C. Montalba. The glowing red-tiled roofs of the old Flemish town of Middelburg, the aspect of quiet and calm at the old sea-

No. 224. *"The Port of Middelburg."* Miss CLARA MONTALBA.

port, with the craft waiting for wind and tide, take us to another atmosphere than English fields. Miss Montalba succeeds in giving us an exact indication of her picture, which is true in local color, and composed, as we see, with great breadth and skill.

Two pictures by Associates of the Academy must be mentioned with the landscapes. Mr. Boughton's scenes in Holland have the advantage of figures in quaint costumes, but, in a *"Quiet Corner of a Garnered Field,"* the interest and beauty are in the treatment of the landscape; so, also, in Mr. Gregory's, entitled *"Startled"*—a little picture of a bank near a wood, with a child startled by a hare—the painting of the bank and the wood must be first considered.

The large landscape (No. 60) sent by Mr. Parsons, studied near Stratford-on-Avon, formed one of the features of the main gallery. The style of the illustrator of so many

No. 60. *"Meadows by the Avon."* ALFRED PARSONS.

publications is well known in black-and-white, but here we have a study of color; sunset light streaming across the meadows, and, in the river on the left, the moon's reflected light. There is a touch of sadness in the picture, as in Mark Fisher's quiet landscape with cattle following a peasant carrying an armful of fresh cuttings through an orchard in Normandy; very natural in action, and harmonious with the blue of the old peasant's dress against the foliage and gray sky.

No 213. *"Homeward."* MARK FISHER.

No. 201. *"A Bed of Water-Lilies."*

KEELEY HALSWELL, A.R.S.A.

No. 52. *"At the Fall of the Leaf."*

W. S. JAY.

No. 156. *"The Shepherd's Return."*

E. A. WATERLOW.

No. 198. *"The Seaweed Harvest."*

HENRY MOORE.

No. 29. *"Tipping a Shrimp-Trawl."* C. NAPIER HEMY.

Sketches of four fine landscapes are placed together on page 164; of Mr. Henry Moore, Keeley Halswelle, E. A. Waterlow, and Mr. W. S. Jay. The first three of these artists we have seen in the notice of the Royal Academy.

Two regular contributors to the exhibitions at the Royal Academy make their appear-

No. 170. *"Coral-Fishing in the Gulf of Salerno."* HAMILTON MACALLUM.

No. 40. "'*Leaves have their Time to fall.*'" DAVID MURRAY, A. R. S. A.

ance this year only at the Grosvenor Gallery. Mr. Hemy paints on the coasts of Devon-
shire and Cornwall, but Mr. Hamilton Macallum chooses more sunny scenes on the coast
of Italy. These painters know the sea, and their pictures are very little idealized. Mr.
Macallum, as a rule, waits and observes until the picture is before him, and studies with
great success the effect of rippling, luminous sea, which he has given us in "*Coral-Fishing*

No. 32. "*Gathering Fuel—Sestri Levante.*" F. W. W. TOPHAM.

32 x 54

No. 157. *"Resting the Deer—Strathyre, Perthshire."*

J. SMART.

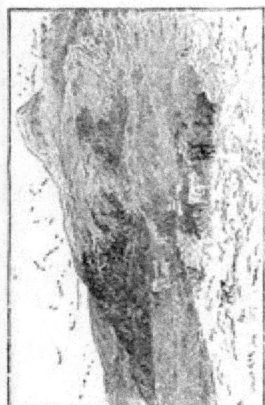

40 x 75

No. 137. *"Lollard's Tower, Lambeth Palace."*

C. E. HOLLOWAY.

"A gray and grief-worn aspect of old days."—BYRON.

20 x 30

No. 182. *"The Old Orchard."*

I. HETHERINGTON.

27 x 48

No. 163. *"Three Fishers."*

EDWARD H. FAHEY.

the Gulf of Salerno." It is no secret that this fine picture was rejected at the Royal Academy. But sea-painters like Hamilton Macallum, C. N. Hemy, and Henry Moore are assured of success, no matter what may befall their works at the hands of the hanging committee, who (in the multitude of pictures sent in every year) sometimes omit important works like the foregoing.

Mr. David Murray's "*Leaves have their Time to fall*" and Mr. Topham's "*Gathering Fuel*" were prominently placed in the Grosvenor Gallery. The subjects are similar, but nothing could be more dissimilar than the treatment of the two pictures; the former, liter-

No. 144. "*Music and Moonlight—Venice.*" T. C. FARRER.

ally, rather coarsely painted, but good in color and drawing; the latter, a picture of Italy in the old familiar colors, with blue distance and picturesque peasantry.

Other landscapes, sketched on page 167, are, "*Resting the Drove*" (No. 157), by J. Smart, a prominent member of the Royal Scottish Academy; a bit of old Lambeth Palace (No. 137), by C. E. Holloway, a good painter of the Thames; "*Three Fishers*," by E. H. Fahey; and "*The Old Orchard*," by I. Hetherington.

Mr. T. C. Farrer has painted a view of Windsor Castle in sunset glow, and another of Venice by moonlight; of the latter he writes: "Every one who has been in Venice will remember the barge that goes out every moonlight night with its load of musicians, and traverses the Grand Canal, stopping at the different hotels and well-known places of resort for foreigners, making the night gay with the sound of music and the flash of the gondoliers' oars." Of the innumerable artists who have chosen this subject, few—from Canaletto to

No. 313. "*Off the Coast of Portugal.*" TRISTRAM ELLIS.

Mr. Farrer—have *quite* succeeded in drawing a gondola; but the main interest here is in the beautiful moonlit sky and the movement on the waters of the Adriatic.

The water-colors at the Grosvenor Gallery never form a very important part of this exhibition. During the lifetime of Richard Doyle, and until last year, this part of the gallery was enlivened with many of his fairy legends and drawings, always full of fancy and humor. Mr. Walter Crane and other water-color artists have contributed, and there are always some interesting examples of the art. Mr. Tristram Ellis sent three drawings this

No. 363. "*Antwerp.*" A. B. DONALDSON.

year, one of which he has sketched; Mr. Donaldson's "*Antwerp*" is a wonderfully airy view across the Scheldt a little after high water. True in tone and good in perspective, this little drawing brings the city before us with great reality.

No. 342. *"By the Wayside."* DAVID BATES.

It is difficult to indicate any of the studies of "still life" in a sketch, but Mr. David Bates has shown us his *"By the Wayside,"* near a wood in an English country lane; *"Meadow-Sweet,"* by Edith Berkley, is a graceful and pretty bit of color; and the *"Twins,"* by S. Berkely, both truthful and humorous: the latter would make a good engraving. There was a small, unimportant portrait in water-colors of Dante Rossetti as a young man, by Holman Hunt; and works by Professor Legros, Stuart Wortley, J. M. Joplin, R. R. Holmes, W. E. F. Britton, Edgar Barclay, Arthur Hughes, Gerald Robinson, Mrs. Stillman, Mrs. Gosse, Mrs. Cecil Lawson, and Mrs. Joplin.

No. 359. *"Meadow-Sweet"* Miss EDITH BERKLEY.

No. 289. *"Twins."* STANLEY BERKLEY.

No. 411. *"A Sonata of Beethoven."* (*Marble statuette.*)
HAMO THORNYCROFT, A. R. A.

The sculpture-gallery included works by J. E. Boehm, R.A., Hamo Thornycroft, A.R.A., Professor Legros, G. B. Amendola, Count Gleichen, T. N. MacLean, E. Onslow Ford, E. R. Mullins, R. B. Browning, Waldo Story, T. S. Lee, Miss Chaplin, Miss Montalba, and

No. 390. *"Meditation."* (*Marble.*)
T. NELSON MACLEAN.

No. 423. *"Study in Bronze."*
R. BARRETT BROWNING.

No. 419.   *"Una Scillans."*   (*Terra-cotta statuette.*)   PEPLOE BROWN.

many others   Mr. R. B. Browning's large bronze statue of Dryope was the prominent object
in the gallery—an unpleasing work, but full of promise and power; and Mr. Thornycroft's
marble statuette of Miss Sassoon one of the best pieces of sculpture of the year.

No. 397.   *"Ethel."*   (*Terra-cotta bust.*)
MISS HENRIETTA MONTALBA.

No. 407.   *"Dryope fascinated by Apollo in the Form of a
Serpent."*   (*Life-size bronze.*)   R. BARRETT BROWNING.

THE INSTITUTE OF PAINTERS IN OIL-COLORS.

No. 278. *"Interior, Peasant's Cottage."*
FREDERICK BROWN.

THE Institute of Painters in Oils, which is an entirely new institution, opened its first exhibition on the 17th of December, 1883, at the new galleries in Piccadilly, with a collection of some eight hundred works in painting and sculpture. This exhibition is annual, and open to all artists, subject to the selection necessary in order to obtain the best works. Mr. J. D. Linton is the president, and there are a hundred and five foundation members.

That there is no feeling of antagonism between the Royal Academy and this society is shown by the number of Academicians and Associates who are either members of the Institute or who contributed to the exhibition. We have selected a few illustrations to give a general idea of the strength of the collection, commencing with a good *genre* picture by Frederick Brown, an artist who made a mark in the Academy in 1883.

Our second sketch (No. 211), "*A Young Tramp*," is by Henry Wells, R.A., one of the elder members of the Royal Academy, the painter of a very large picture of men and horses, "*Loading at a Quarry*," in the Academy, and of several portraits this year. The artist has here found as an excellent subject for his pencil the head of some wild, untutored, but intelli-

gent-looking young savage, whose face might well arouse the benevolent feelings of the phi-
lanthropist. It requires no seer to predict that a mind like that of this poor lad's might,
with proper cultivation, produce the fruits of a great and noble life. There is little exaggera-

No. 211. "*A Young Tramp*." HENRY T. WELLS, R. A.

tion of refinement in the presentment of this London "gamin," one of the "waifs and strays"
of cities; from a philanthropic point of view, we should be disposed to pronounce this "one
of the best portraits of the year."

Mr. J. E. Hodgson, R. A., is another member of the Academy whose work does not
appear in the early part of this book, but it would not be complete without one of Mr.
Hodgson's Eastern studies. Here is an incident in the late war in the East—a group consisting of three Turks, in their Eastern home, entertaining a couple of "Jack Tars." The
sailor's habit of making himself at home under all circumstances is amusingly depicted in
two "man-of-war's men": one is seen seated crossed-legged upon a divan, holding in one
hand a long Turkish pipe, and in the other a cup of sweet coffee, while his comrade
endeavors to look as little like "a fish out of water" as circumstances will permit; the
staid, sober-minded Easterns listen with dignified courtesy to the remarks of their novel
guests. The design is full of quiet humor, the painting firm, and the details are given with
great accuracy. Looking at this sketch, we are brought very closely to the spirit of Mr.

Hodgson's work; imagination must picture the rich yet subdued colors of the robes of the Turks and their surroundings.

Mr. Pettie's larger works we have already noticed, but the sketch of this single-figure subject will give an idea of another phase of his art, in which quality and finish are more considered. No. 474, "*Sweet Seventeen*," by John Pettie, R. A., is evidently the artist's *beau-idéal* of fair girlhood—one in whom the light of life and happiness is bright. In color, this was a charming picture, graceful and easy in posture, the white neck-handkerchief with its adornment of a simple red rose, and even her powdered tresses, giving a piquant freshness to the face and form. We imagine this is one of those fancy portraits Mr. Pettie has more than once painted with marked success, and which have been afterward engraved; but it is not equal in interest to "*Her Grace*," painted in 1881, and now familiar as an etching.

No. 441. "*East and West.*" J. E. Hodgson, R. A.

No. 446, "*Well-known Footsteps*," by Alma-Tadema, R. A. With this artist's name appended to the picture, it is hardly necessary to add that the treatment of the subject is classical. Seated upon a cushioned bench, in an apartment leading to the entrance to her mansion, a fair Greek girl rests with her arm upon a leopard's skin, while she leans forward, listening for the familiar foot-fall of one who is expected. In the open doorway, through which the sun is shining brightly, some one is advancing, laden with a magnificent offering of roses and beyond is a bright peep of garden-ground. The picture is quite a little gem,

No. 474. "*Sweet Seventeen*" J. PETTIE, R. A.

the girl's expectant figure gracefully posed, while her form is hidden in semi-shadow, which makes the peep of sunlight more tellingly effective. The sketch indicates well the type of faces and the curious treatment of the subject—a style and period with which Mr. Tadema has made us all familiar.

Mrs. Alma-Tadema paints in the same studio, but it can not be said that she borrows her art from her husband. In No. 196, "*A Bible-Lesson*," the style she has struck out for herself is peculiarly her own, and her designs, while they often convey a lesson, are generally happy combinations of domestic and picturesque life. In the daintily painted little *genre* picture before us, a handsomely dressed old lady is seen engaged in teaching her little grand-daughter Scripture lessons in the stories represented on the blue tiles with which the walls

No. 446. "*Well-known Footsteps.*" L. Alma-Tadema, R. A.

are adorned. Mrs. Tadema is more reticent in color than her husband, but, like him, she spares no pains in the execution of her work, and considers no detail or accessory too insignificant to be painted with care. Note, for instance, the introduction of the grand-mother's chair and foot-stool in the distance, how it adds to the interest of the picture and balances the composition.

No. 611, "*A'lea*," by Edwin Long, R. A. One of the Eastern figures which this artist has now for some years made his more particular study. (See page 12.)

No. 101, "*The Blue Girl*," by P. R. Morris, A. R. A. This artist, who has been very successful in his treatment of portraits of children, here pictures a funny little figure of a

23

girl in blue hood and dress, seated in a wood with a half-peeled orange in her lap. Upon her right is an object not indicated in the sketch—a rabbit seated at the entrance of its burrow, the timid animal apparently not at all frightened at her little ladyship. The original is remarkable for pretty expression and childish character; the scheme of color blue, orange, and black.

No. 320, "*Dog-Days*," by R. W. Macbeth, A.R.A. Two young ladies seated at table, and apparently wholly free from fear of that terrible bugbear, "hydrophobia," for the name

No. 196. "*A Bible-Lesson.*" Mrs. Alma-Tadema.

of their canine favorites arranged before them is legion. The artist's sketch indicates the central group. We have spoken of Mr. Macbeth's art elsewhere.

No. 447, "*The Rialto Market*," by Henry Woods, A.R.A. This artist, who is brother-in-law to Luke Fildes, A.R.A., is one of that little coterie, Van Haanen, De Blaas, Logsdail, and a few others, who have taken up their residence in Venice, where they appear to be founding what may be considered a new modern school of art. As far as Mr. Woods is concerned, the Venetian scenes, which he is constantly reproducing, are really Venice of

NO. 6II.   "*Klea.*"   EDWIN LONG, R. A.

the present day—Venice in all her brightness and beauty, painted in a conscientious spirit, and with the thoroughness and skill which have earned for him a reputation in a few years, and his election to the rank of an Associate of the Academy. In the "*Rialto Market,*" the girl seated on the right is just one of dozens of such figures one sees daily in the city; and

No. 101. *"Blue Girl."* Philip Morris, A. R. A.

the bridge itself, the awning over the figure of the girl, etc., are photographically accurate. It will be seen at once by the sketch what a chance for a painter there is here, in sunny

No. 329. *"Dog-Days."* R. W. Macbeth, A. R. A., R. I., M.

effects and variety of rich colors. No wonder English artists linger in Venice, painting subjects of which the art-world seems never to have enough!

No. 227, *"Caterpillars,"* by E. J. Gregory, A. R. A. This study is principally an exercise in color, as we observe in the little girl's red velvet frock, the brick wall, and in the various shades of leafage, in which the young lady is industriously engaged catching caterpillars.

No. 447. *"The Rialto Market."* H. Woods, A. R. A.

A trivial subject and without much grace, but the touch of genius is here, as in all of Mr. Gregory's work. The natural attitude of the child is expressed exactly in the artist's sketch.

The next two clever *genre* pictures indicate a style of art much in repute at the galleries of the Institute: the first, No. 152, *"The Pride of her Heart,"* by Hugh Cameron, a young mother delightedly playing with her little son upon her lap; and No. 749, *"A Portrait,"* by E. Lintz—a capital picture of a little girl seated upon a chair, holding a dreadfully fat, over-pampered pug-dog on her lap. It may be hard to say which of the pair is the *"Portrait"* alluded to in the title of the work, but one is quite sure which *portrait* will be preferred.

No. 227. *"Caterpillars."* E. J. Gregory, A.R.A., R.I., M.

No. 152. *"The Pride of her Heart."*
Hugh Cameron, M.

No. 749. *"A Portrait."*
E. Lantz

No. 672, "*In the Nick of Time*," by R. C. Woodville. Our illustration gives the principal figure in one of this artist's usually stirring war-subjects. It is an incident in the recent Egyptian war. Some of Arabi's soldiers have laid a train to blow up a bridge by which the communications of the army were maintained, and, while just in the act of putting a fuse to the powder, they are disturbed by a patrol of troopers, who, galloping down to the

No. 672. "*In the Nick of Time.*" R. C. WOODVILLE, R. I., M.

spot, discover the enemy in the act. The saber makes short work of the offenders, who attempt to flee in different directions, some boldly taking to the river with their horses, while one man still persists in his attempt to fire the train, and the trooper in the sketch is defeating the effort. There is always plenty of dash and "go" in Mr. Woodville's work, and lovers of military incidents will be delighted with this spirited sketch.

No. 122, "*The Daylight dies*," by Alfred Parsons. As is the case with much of this artist's work, his picture here is a poem. The subject is simple enough—a river with sedgy banks, a peep of meadows, and a few trees and shrubs, but the scene is lighted with that

No. 122. "*The Daylight dies.*" ALFRED PARSONS, R. I., *M.*

mystical, half-defined light which just precedes the time when the setting sun leaves Nature to the reign of another luminary, and to the darkness which is in harmony with the idea of rest. We really know of no landscape-painter who more faithfully or fully interprets

FRIENDLY ADVANCES.
J. P. Beadle.

Nature in her various times and moods than Mr. Parsons. He ignores, as in the work we are referring to, all attempts at dramatic display or picture-making, and, with the simple purpose of realizing Nature in the mood in which she is presenting herself to his mind, he transfers with peculiar power that mental vision to canvas. There is no need of Mr. Abbey's figures to aid the sentiment of this picture.

No. 508. *"The Window-Seat."* FRANCIS D. MILLET.

Another artist, perhaps better known in America than in England, is Francis D. Millet. *'The Window-Seat"* (No. 508) is rich in the charm of light and graceful movement. It is almost the invariable rule that an artist is in after-life influenced by the art of his master; but this is not so with Mr. Millet, who is certainly original in his method of work. In

24

the picture we are commenting upon, one finds no trace of the manner of either De
Keyser or Van Lerius, and there is something peculiarly happy in the thought of this fair

No. 261. "*A Yorkshire Fisher-Girl.*" W. SMALL.

young figure seated, bathed in sunshine, as she plies needle and thread. There is a style
about this picture which the artist has made his own.

One of the most able draughtsmen in England, one whose work is too seldom seen on
canvas, is Mr. William Small. In 1876 he made an impression by a large and powerful

figure-picture entitled "*The Wreck*," sent to the Royal Academy. Since that time he has exhibited smaller paintings, generally of sea-coast scenes, but is best known by his numerous illustrations on wood. Like his contemporaries, Charles Green, F. Barnard, and E. A. Abbey, his time is nearly all taken up with drawings in black-and-white. No. 261, "*A Yorkshire Fisher-Girl*," a study of a north-country lassie with a basket of fish balanced on her head, knitting as she goes, is as bright, fresh, and airy as anything from his hand, but the exigencies of book-illustration in England take from us probably many good painters, such as Mr. Small and Mr. Randolph Caldecott.

No. 375, "*The Humming-Top*," by Joseph Clark. Two cottage children watching a top spin. The artist here exhibits, as usual, much insight of childish character. This little pict-

No. 375. "*The Humming-Top.*" J. CLARK, M.

ure, like Mr. Clark's former works, "*The Bird's Nest*," "*The Empty Cradle*," and "*The Sick Child*," is treated with feeling and skill, redeeming the subjects from any charge of puerility. Thus M. Edouard Frère has painted in France for forty years.

No. 532, "*Mrs. Betsy Criddle's School*," by Frederick G. Cotman. A dame's school, with the old schoolmistress teaching a little boy his letters. There is always something suggestive when old and young are brought together, and never more so than when obeying a first principle of nature, such as age imparting instruction to youth. Mr. Cotman's design is distinguished for unity of purpose, and for a realization of character that is both interesting and impressive.

No. 187. "*She loved him for the Perils he had passed,*" by Charles J. Staniland. Stories of dangers by flood and field have always been dear to maiden heart; and the tall soldier seated on the window-sill, recounting his adventures to the comely but rather Puritan-looking Less before him, gives point to his history in that he himself is wounded. A stray bullet or well-aimed sword-cut has injured his right arm, so that his account of bloody fights and hair-breadth escapes has illustration in his own maimed person. The subject, it

No. 532. "*Mrs. Betsy Creddle's School.*" F. G. Cotman, R. I., M.

is true, is but a love-story; still, it is love founded on admiration of courage and acts of personal valor, qualities which should have some weight as an assurance of future happiness for the young couple.

The four pictures sketched on page 190 are by skilled artists. Mr. Ernest Crofts is a battle-painter, lately elected to the rank of Associate of the Academy. No. 251, "*The Old Home,*" by G. G. Kilburne, pictures some wanderer in the rough ways of life, who, carrying her sorrow huddled up in her shawl, returns in the winter snows, to peep in at the warmly-lighted rooms of the old home. No. 687, "*Cromwell at Bootham Bar,*" by Ernest Crofts, A. R. A. The Protector, with a knight and armed train, filing from the castle. No. 479, "*Taken to the Road,*" by Charles Cattermole. A study of a young man, mounted on a useful-looking hack, who, whether from folly, fate, or misfortune, has betaken himself to the disgraceful life of a highwayman. No. 714, *"For whom, and from whom?"* by Haynes Williams. A highly-finished sketch of the cavalier in the artist's picture of this subject.

No. 187. *"She loved him for the Perils he had passed."* C. J. STANILAND, R. I., *M.*

No. 178, *"The Marsh-King's Daughter,"* by John Scott. The artist, who is fond of the mysticism of legendary lore, has here another illustration of the subject he exhibited in the Royal Academy. The incident is taken from one of Hans Andersen's charming fairy-tales. The stork recounts the scene: "This evening," he says, "I went among the rushes, and while I was there three swans came; one of them threw off her plumage, and I immediately recognized her as one of the princesses of our home in Egypt. There she sat

No. 251. "*The Old Home*."
G. G. Kilburne, R. I., M.

No. 687. "*Cromwell at Basham Bar*."
Ernest Crofts, A. R. A.

No. 479. "*Taken to the Road*."
Charles Cattermole, R. I., M.

No. 714. "*For whom, and from whom?*"
Haynes Williams, M.

without any covering but her long black hair. The two swans rose up with her plumage."
Mr. Scott represents the marsh-king's daughter seated, with a regal air, upon the roots of
a tree, below her a pool covered with water-lilies, and at her side the curious, councilor-like-
looking birds.

No. 197. *"Highland Eagles and Red-Deer Calf,"* by Samuel Carter. Since the death
of Sir Edwin Landseer, Mr. Carter has certainly proved himself to be one of our best

No. 178. *"The Marsh-King's Daughter."* John Scott

painters of deer. Keeping these animals constantly about him at his own home, he is
enabled to study closely their habits and daily life. The subject of our illustration tells its

own story. By some mischance a young deer has, all untimely, met with death. It may have slipped and fallen from some mountain-height; or, it may be possible that

> ". . . a shot, at random sent,
> Found mark the archer little meant";

but, be that as it may, the graceful animal now forms a prey for that king of birds, the eagle. Two of these birds have swooped down from their lofty flight, and wait but a moment ere they commence their meal. Not only has Mr. Carter pictured with power the birds and animal, but one feels also a sense of the desolate grandeur of the mountain-heights.

No. 197. *"Highland Eagles and Red-Deer Calf."* Samuel Carter, M.

THE WATER-COLOR SOCIETIES.*

THE art of water-color painting is essentially of English practice, but it is not, as many people suppose it to be, of English origin. Few, indeed, have been the arts that have leaped complete into life. Generally the development has been gradual, and the progress slow. And this has been the case with water-color. It was practiced, tentatively, even as long ago as in the day of Albert Dürer. It was brought in a measure to perfection in the seventeenth century in Holland, but the method of its employment there was limited. It was used chiefly, and used beautifully, in the rare drawings by Adrian van Ostade and Cornelius Dusart, which record a vulgar life with delicate brush. And the French *gouache* of the eighteenth century—the *gouache* of Baudouin and Lavreince—has something in common with the English art of water-color which was practiced contemporaneously with it. These things it is fair to recall and chronicle, though the mention of them detracts in no wise from the merit of the English school. For, after all, however important be the language of an art, far more important is the message which sooner or later that language is trusted to deliver. And, if the formation of the language of water-color is in truth but in part ours, its message is wholly our own. It is as practiced by the greater English masters—by Turner, by Girtin, by Cotman, by David

No. 228. *"Is the Change right?"*
E. BUCKMAN.

* The sketches interspersed over the following pages will serve to remind the reader of some water-color artists, of whom it has been impossible to speak in this year's English art. On the other hand, some important paintings are mentioned, and not sketched, it being impossible to render the effects of some water-colors in a sketch in black and white in line.—ED.

25

Cox, by Dewint—that water-color has contributed so much to the pleasures of the drawing-room and the picture-gallery, and has furthered and widened our interest in the world
of nature.

In England, too, as elsewhere beforehand, the beginnings were tentative and timid; but
in England the result was to be a success, not only assured, but of long duration and of
wide extent.

No. **194**. *"The Sisters."* E. K. Johnson.

It is said that the demand, early or in the middle of the eighteenth century, among us
for views of English castles, country-houses, and cathedral towns, stimulated our practice of
water-color. Capable draughtsmen visited town after town, country-seat after country-seat,
and to the accurate work of the pencil added washes of color. The color at first was

hardly more than neutral tint. Local hues were at first avoided. But gradually they crept in; and presently, too, the impression of atmospheric effect—the changes of the light and air—came to be added to the record of permanent form. Thus did pure topographical art give place to art proper. Thus was Sandby succeeded by Turner, Marlow by Girtin.

No. 88. "*The Morning Chat: on the Seine, Paris.*" BASIL BRADLEY.

At last English water-color art was so far developed that its practitioners—very few of whom were likewise painters in oil—resolved and were able to found a society which should invite the public to annual exhibitions. And thus, in the year 1805, there came to be established that Society of Painters in Water-Colors which continues to this day its honorable or respectable career. To it, almost at the beginning, belonged John Varley, an artist always learned and at first simple. He did much for the development of the art. To it belonged, before the society had existed many years, painters as different and as eminent as Prout and William Hunt. And in 1818 there was experienced the need of a second society, and thereupon what was then called the "new" society came to be founded. That society is now the "Institute," and of it and of its exhibition I shall speak further on. We will first, however, visit the older gallery in Pall Mall East. Upon both bodies royal favor, as well as popular appreciation, has been bestowed. They are, of late, the "Royal" Society and the "Royal" Institute.

The Royal Society of Painters in Water-Colors is presided over by the veteran artist, Sir John Gilbert, whose one contribution this year is sketched by himself in this work.

This exhibition is held in a single convenient gallery, approached by entrance through the pretty stone frontage designed by the late Mr. Cockerell. It is confessedly a close body; that is, to its recurrent shows none but members and associates may contribute. It has thirty-five members and about as many associates. The members govern the whole action of the society; the associates are in a sense probationers; from their ranks members are chosen, and, until an associate becomes a member, his function is but to exhibit. Then, of course, there are a few honorary members, of whom Mr. Ruskin is one. And Mr. Ruskin sometimes annoys the over-sensitive critic by the exhibition of that which the critic is sorry to see; and sometimes Mr. Ruskin delights alike the critic, the artists, and the cultivated public by the exhibition of an architectural study wrought with singular refinement of hand, in obedience to the dictates of a delicate and a subtly observant eye. But of course it is

No. 10. "*Timon and Apemantus.*" (*Timon of Athens.*) Sir John Gilbert, R. A.

not upon the honorary members that there falls the heavy business of assuring the main interest of the show. Certain of the elder regular members have long been able to take that burden on their shoulders with fair chance of success. There is George Fripp, for instance; there is Alfred Hunt; there is G. P. Boyce; and there is Carl Haag. Still, it has to be allowed that at least one or two of these gentlemen—all of whom have reached, and

some of whom have passed, late middle life—have waxed a little indolent or a little weary,
Mr. Boyce, whose drawings of old buildings (notably one called "*Where Bridewell stood*,"
exhibited many years ago) gave him a great and deserved reputation, puts in an appearance
—or at all events a prominent appearance—but rarely.

Of the men I have thus far named, Carl Haag is, at this moment, the surest pillar of
the house. He is, as his name implies, by birth a German, but he came to England now

No. 109. "*Silk and Calico Bazaar, Cairo.*" E. A. GOODALL.

very many years ago, loving the country and loving its practice of water-color. He is
Hofmaler to the Duke of Saxe-Coburg and Gotha, and a deserved favorite of English
royalty. He exhibited in Pall Mall the records of his travels in the East. He had
explored Egypt before Gérôme. He had followed in the steps of William Müller, an artist
of extraordinary vigor, especially in landscape. But Carl Haag is a more elaborate painter
and a finer draughtsman of the human frame than Müller ever was. And he has never
been seen in greater perfection than in the exhibition of 1884. His chief work is his most

alistic vision of one stage of the long journey which the faithful Eliezer took with Rebecca when he brought her on a camel's back to be the bride of Isaac. Eliezer has been a successful man. He marches solidly along, full of the consciousness of Abraham's approval when he reaches home. And the young woman—those gold coins pendent above the forehead (they are the "engaged ring" of Eastern society, Mr. Haag tells me, the coins

No. 47. *"But the Word of the Lord endureth forever."* R. BARNES.

that mark her betrothal) jingle pleasantly in her ears, and she knows that she is not likely to be disappointing. Never did camel step so delicately, yet with proper pride in the triumph he shares; never were Eastern textures and gay trappings richer or more rare.

Mr. Alfred Hunt deserves mention next, I think, and not because he is an Oxford man of mark, a scholar, a philosophical Liberal, interested genuinely in politics and social progress, a member of the Athenæum Club. All that must be very interesting and satisfactory to Mr. Hunt and his friends, but it has little bearing on his work as an artist. As an artist he has studied two things—not necessarily incompatible. He has studied nature and Turner. He is Turner's disciple. Rarely does he produce a single delicate drawing which does not display the influence to which he has mainly leaned. No one is more industrious, no one more patient, no one more enamored of the beauty of his subjects or more aware of their inevitable difficulties. Alfred Hunt is perhaps, above all things, a painter of atmosphere. In this year's exhibition, his "*Deserted River-Bed*" portrayed, indeed, no land of exceptional charm, but a sky crowded with interest, and dealt with by the hand of a poet.

Mr. Albert Goodwin, a younger artist, but a worker in the same field, is one of the most rising members of the Royal Society. He is one of those men to whose work we look first for the charm of originality, freshness—poetry combined with power. He is faulty —sometimes apt to be exaggerated in the rendering of effects that stir him—but he is almost always impressive. The seaboard town of Whitby, which Mr. Hunt has painted so often with exquisite refinement, Mr. Goodwin painted last year with extraordinary vigor. Mr. Hunt achieved subtilty and the rendering of many facts; Mr. Goodwin's was the more direct and decisive record of a prompt vision. And this year his "*Sunset in the Manufacturing Districts*" is as fine as his "*Whitby*" and as fine as his "*Last of the Armada*—the

No. 28. "*Fighting the Sea: Yarmouth Tug saving a Dismasted Fishing-Smack.*" OSWALD W. BRIERLY.

skeleton of the last ship, the bare ribs on the wild coast. Poetry of a grim and potent and portentous sort is in this "*Sunset in the Manufacturing Districts.*" Before us lies the desolate, spoiled country that a feebler artist would avoid, because it has lost its prettiness; that the more vigorous artist would enjoy, because it has gained its sentiment and its experience. A deserted house, the ruin of a modern builder, is quite in the foreground, and waste land that was country once and is hardly yet town. "The grass grows scant as hair in leprosy," writes Mr. Browning of some such place. Beyond lie the houses closely packed, and the smoky steamers of a tidal river; then the flats, and then perhaps the sea. But over all this, which is so sordid and squalid and yet so pathetic besides, the weird drama of sunset is enacted in the sky. Great wreaths of cloud, strange in color and savage and

No. 95.   "*A Dorsetshire Stream.*"   WILMOT PILSBURY.

threatening in form, are dragged over the placidness of the upper heavens. A fine imagination dictated this work, and dictated it with all the more of clearness and of force because its subject was of no remote origin, but was found at our very doors, in the work-a-day England which we know.

Mr. Herbert Marshall—with his "*From Hyde Park Corner, looking west,*" and his "*And all that Mighty Heart is lying still*"—is likewise a painter of the modern world, of modern cities. And so sometimes is Mr. Hale. And Mr. Hale is truly refined. His observation is subtile; it is not mechanical and photographic. I can not myself assign to Mr. Marshall quite so high a place. Still, the "*From Hyde Park Corner, looking west,*" is undoubtedly striking. I wish only that the painter's vision of the modern world, to which he wisely betakes himself, were in itself more artistic. He paints skillfully what he sees, but he sees too much what everybody sees. An artist of mark must be fresh.

Now, Mr. Thorne Waite—another of the younger men—brings a certain amount of freshness to the treatment of themes in the original choice of which he had doubtless felt the influence of Dewint. Mr. Thorne Waite's "*Loiterers*" is by no means the largest, but it is assuredly the most perfect and most harmonious drawing in the exhibition. If, like a new associate, Mr. Pilsbury, Mr. Waite here recalls Mr. Birket Foster—that veteran miniaturist in water-color, who is still almost a leading man in the Royal Society—it is but for a moment. Generally Mr. Waite is either wholly original or wholly a follower of Dewint; and, like Dewint, he paints the English lowlands, or, like Hine of the Institute, the Downs of Sussex.

Another painter of pure landscape should perhaps be mentioned here, before we pass on to those who paint chiefly the shore and sea, or chiefly the figure, draped or undraped, and that is Mr. J. W. North. He is, perhaps, our most delicate painter of delicate foliage

No. 40. "*Clearing the Wreck: Tide rising.*" R. BEAVIS.

—and of the play of atmosphere upon it, in limited spaces—and "*My Garden Hedge, my Orchard Fence*" (a study of nasturtium and apples) is certainly a quite lovely rendering of a tangle of greenery and full-colored blossom.

Miss Clara Montalba's "*Souvenir of Middelburg*"—golden and red—reminds us that she, who is perhaps the most gifted member of an unquestionably gifted family, is, in a sense, a

painter of landscape. But it is the waters, and especially the Venetian waters, and the wide
sky that is seen from the gondola shooting over the lagoon, that is her proper province,
and so Miss Montalba may be fairly mentioned now that we have come among the painters of the coast and sea. The essential quality of her work is perhaps the quality of spirit-

No. 140. *"The Deserter."* CHARLES GREGORY.

edness. It is so far vigorous that it is almost masculine; nay, it may be pronounced masculine without any qualification of the word. But it is a little wont to be sketchy, not alone
in touch but likewise in conception. Its composition is sometimes incomplete, and it is
never intricate. Still, it is remarkable work, so vivid, fresh, and free. Unity of impression
is at all events never sacrificed in it to the accumulation of detail.

Among the most notable painters of coast and ship and sea are Mr. Henry Moore, Mr.
Powell, and Mr. Oswald Brierly. Mr. Brierly is essentially a draughtsman of all the detail
of ships, a naval rather than a true marine painter, and bold rather than subtile or various.
Henry Moore is devoted to the record of the waves as they beat upon the shore. He is
an artist more careful to preserve refinement than to display strength. He is various, but
most interesting to us when he betakes himself to the Mediterranean blue. Mr. Powell,
whose large drawing of waves and sky occupied one of the places of honor in this gallery,
has for years been a great yachting-man. Round the Scottish coasts, where his home is, he

has been everywhere and he has seen everything. And he has seen the world at unusual hours. He has caught Nature unawares. He paints the sea in days of endless mist, when nothing seems to change, and when all is harmonious and placid. He paints effects which before him have had no charm for any one—effects which escaped not, perhaps, the observation but certainly the *interested* observation of Turner. But of the marine painters of the day he is certainly one of the most valuable.

It is generally agreed that the Society of Painters in Water-Colors is least strong in figure-painters; but it has had, and still has, many notable men as members. It is now many years since young Burne-Jones was practically excluded (the council of the year

No. 24. *"A Capture."* NORMAN TAYLER.

declining some of his works); and, since Sir Frederick Burton seceded in consequence of that decision, a little of the Philistine spirit must surely have existed in a society which could take exception to the refined and poetical drawings of Mr. Burne-Jones. But in those days the landscape-painters had the strongest voice at the council, and the figure-painter was at a discount. The old society is still faithful to its traditions, but there is certainly an increase in the encouragement which the Royal Society affords to figure-painters. The recent elections of Mr. Albert Moore, Mr. Du Maurier, and Mr. Henshall prove this unmistakably. And the popularity of Mrs. Allingham's pretty work is noteworthy. It is true that Mr. Du Maurier could hardly *paint* a figure when he was elected, but he could, at all events,

"*The Corn-Market, Abbeville.*"   SAMUEL J. HODSON.

draw one.   And the society was right to give him welcome, and he has justified what I may call the eagerness, if I may not call it the prematureness, of his choice.   For, since then, the fashionable artist of "Punch"—the elegant and piquant draughtsman with pen and

No. 30.   "*From Hyde Park Corner, looking west.*"   HERBERT M. MARSHALL.

ink—has labored much at water-color. A certain art of comedy attends his performances generally, but in this year's picture, "*The Peacock and the Nightingale*," the comedy is slight. It is rather a moral tale—the tale of the triumph of simple charm over much-

"*Souvenir of Middelburg.*" CLARA MONTALBA.

adorned and self-conscious beauty. The scene is "in society"; London society in our own day spreading pretty widely, and the fashionable young man no longer bound by the restrictions laid upon him in the days of Mr. Thackeray. He may venture, now, "north of

No. 100. "*The Cid and the Five Moorish Kings*" (*vide Lockhart's "Spanish Ballads"*). W. E. LOCKHART, R.S.A.

Oxford Street," without fear of losing his way. This time, in Mr. Du Maurier's drawing, he is quite at home at Hampstead, four miles north of London. I think he is in Mr. Du Maurier's own abode; for there is the manly figure of a young gentleman, with whom Mr. Du Maurier is very intimately connected, and there, too—not to speak of the ladies—is Mr. Henry James, surely; and there, too, a neighbor, Mr. Alfred Ainger, the "reader" at the Temple. Others, likewise, of the Hampstead world. All is graceful, full of character, full of social charm, and the charm of simplicity is not wholly wanting.

No. 157. *"Signals of Distress."* A. Hopkins.

Mr. Arthur Hopkins's very powerful drawing, called "*Signals of Distress*," is a replica of his picture exhibited in the Royal Academy in 1879, and also recalls another picture entitled "*The Wreck*," by Mr. William Small, in the Academy in 1876. Neither Mr. Small nor Mr. Hopkins has yet distinguished himself as a colorist, but both are most skillful draughtsmen, and have seized the dramatic element with great force. Such work appeals powerfully to islanders whose shores are strewed with wrecks.

What a different world is that of Mr. Albert Moore—the world of vivified Greek sculpture, of lovely fabrics laid over noble forms, as the figures stretch themselves with splendid *insouciance* or repose in a quietude on which "society" makes no claims, and with

which it has nothing to do! Mr. Albert Moore is quite fresh to water-color, but his freshness is that of a master—his work has none of the heaviness or of the over-precision which
is sometimes to be traced in the drawings of an artist in oil betaking himself for the first
time to water-color. He affords us no surprise, and, if he does not fall below his habitual
level in *technique*, it will hardly be asked of him that he shall rise above it. And, in subject, too, if his ideal is a limited ideal (generally that of a single female figure in repose),
it is yet perfectly attained. Here are the pretty draperies again, and the flower-pots in

No. 59. *"The Strollers: the Pet of the Company."* F. BUCKMAN.

which the flowers are ever fresh, and the young women who lounge to right or to left, and
are ever indolent yet ever robust. Of the imitation of an every-day nature there is almost
nothing; but what an admirable art supplants the every-day nature Mr. Moore contentedly
banishes!

We will go back for a moment to some of the elder painters—proficient in styles
brought to perfection now many years ago. There is Mr. Frederick Tayler, for instance,
and there is the president, Sir John Gilbert. Mr. Frederick Tayler's treatment of the figure

"*Calling Hounds out of Cover.*"   FREDERICK TAYLER.

No. 286. "*Ladies' Tresses.*" F. SMALLFIELD.

QUEEN OF THE MAY.
H. SCHMALZ.

is pretty much confined to the hunting-field, but his figures in their association with the horses and the dogs give us the quaintest and the most spirited pictures of one side of English rural life. Nor, of course, is Sir John Gilbert exclusively a figure-painter. He is

No. 247. *"A Street Altar."* L. ALMA-TADEMA, R. A.

skilled in the art of placing his noble troopers or his ragged camp-followers—the van and rear of a great army, chiefly of Puritan and Cavalier times—in the midst of a savage and impressive country, a land of riven oak-tree and blasted heath, and over that country sweeps a wind from the west. If the landscape is a little less natural than David Cox's—if it is

17

less truly studied—it sometimes, for awhile, is as impressive. But this year Sir John Gilbert is, perhaps, hardly at his strongest; and Mr. Frederick Tayler—well, vivacious as he is, we might have said before that he has long been a veteran.

Hardly among the elders, yet not among the juniors, we must name Mr. J. D. Watson, Mr. Smallfield, Mr. E. K. Johnson, and Mr. Henry Wallis. Mr. J. D. Watson has been an excellent character-painter, and this year three drawings prove him to have lost much less of his art than there had lately been some cause to fear. I do not know that Mr. Small-field's "*Ladies Tresses*" is very characteristic, but the reproduction here shows it to be at least decidedly attractive. Mr. E. K. Johnson can be just as immediately attractive as Mr. Smallfield, and perchance he is more deeply refined. He is the painter of many pretty things (see sketch on page 194), but of nothing that is prettier than his blonde, square-cheeked damsels dressed in white. What more charming, for instance, than his "*First Spring Flowers*"—the girl bending over the table with primroses? Mr. Wallis—whom I some-how named with this group—is noticeable not alone for the qualities of color and of grace which he gets into his work in water-color, but also because he is quite an exception to the usual rule, by which—at least from David Cox's days to J. D. Linton's—a painter painting both in oil- and water-colors has generally begun with water-colors and taken subsequently to oils. Mr. Wallis, beginning with oils, has now for some years taken to water-colors. His "*Death of Chatterton*" was famous long before he dreamed of being elected an Associate of the Society of Painters in Water-Colors.

No. 142. "*Tympanistria.*"
EDWARD RADFORD.

Mr. E. J. Poynter, R.A., and Mr. Edward Radford represent well enough by "*Psyche*" and by "*Tympanistria*" the tendency of certain men of taste still to seek classic themes in their treatment of the figure. They are never encumbered nor attracted much by acces-sories. The figure is their proper function. Mr. Poynter does not often depart from his legitimate business of drawing it well, and Mr. Radford draws it seductively. Mr. Alma-Tadema is a classic likewise, and in his "*Street Altar*" the sobriety of the antique street is made only the more pleasantly evident by the permitted but limited inroad of blue sky and blinding sun. Mr. E. F. Brewtnall is another figure-painter whose work in this gallery should be mentioned.

Mr. Buckman treats his figure subjects with humor, if not precisely with beauty, and is a student of character, a fresh observer of the every-day world, more than a great colorist. "*Is the Change right?*" which is sketched on the first page of this chapter, gives a good

No. 203. "*Thoughts.*" J. H. HENSHALL.

idea of his style. But Mr. Henshall, with his large drawing called "*Thoughts,*" No. 203, makes a good display, in the present exhibition, of what can be done with modern dress when it is seen by an artistic eye. He paints a very real young woman, seated in a free-and-easy way on a tall stool in a library. She is not very pretty—not prettier than you ought fairly

to be when a girl is seventeen, and has nothing to trouble her—but he has taken careful
note of her points, and he spares us no engaging turn of the arm, no line that can be
caught in the flow of the shapely figure. A poorer painter would have made the thing
meretricious. Mr. Henshall has so much enjoyed the flexibility of the model, the opportunity she has afforded him for the tracing of a subtile contour, and the play of light and
shade about her dress, that the consequent excellence of his workmanship has given the
picture dignity. It is exactly the kind of work that is certain to appear vulgar and commonplace to spectators on whom the Fates have not bestowed the power to observe, but
in truth it addresses itself with dexterity to some of the most difficult and some of the
most pressing of the problems of art.

Some sixty years ago there was founded the second English Water-Color Society—the
"new society," or, as it is now called, the Royal Institute. It was for many years distinctly
inferior to the elder body, and, under various vicissitudes of fortune, it occupied, until a
year or two since, a somewhat undignified, not to say tunnel-like, gallery, opposite Marlbor-

No. 550. "*A Thrilling Drama.*" WILLIAM L. THOMAS, R. I.

ough House. Of late, however, its affairs have been administered by able and spirited men,
so that in the last days in the old gallery one was certain to see an interesting exhibition
representing the most modern side of English water-color, and especially rich in drawings of

the figure. And the spirit of its administration has been as modern as the style of its work. It conferred, a few years since, upon the whole of its associates the full privileges of membership—including, I believe, for a while, the privilege of paying for its support. For the Institute was a good deal deserted of the public. Its best artists could always sell their

No. 1000. *"Cromwell at Naseby Field."* CHARLES CATTERMOLE.

pictures, but they could sell better, perhaps, in their studios than in their gallery. The popular shilling tinkled with rarity into the money-box. It was time that something was done. The members of the Institute were men of initiative. They devised a scheme by aid of which long life, as a corporate body, could be guaranteed them, and a service rendered to the art of water-color. The funds were forthcoming with which to build a sumptuous gallery in Piccadilly. Space, it was decided, should be allotted with a liberal hand to outsiders; and, moreover, the number of members, whose works were shown inevitably, should be appreciably increased. This has been done with success, and the present year witnessed the second exhibition of the new " Royal Institute," in the palatial yet appropriate abode designed by Mr. Robson, the distinguished architect, which is now one of the features of Piccadilly.

The Institute has, during the last few years, been rich in figure-subjects. Its president, Mr. James Linton, is one of the most eminent figure-painters of the English school. He

No. 613.   *"Priscilla."*   JAMES D. LINTON, *President.*

is an exquisite draughtsman, but above all a draughtsman of the figure in picturesque costume, and he is a most rich and harmonious colorist. Some appreciative critics of his work like him best when he is devoted to a single figure. It is then, perhaps, that his touch is most faultless, and his expression of textures, including the lovely texture of the flesh most irreproachable. And this year he is represented by a single figure—the Puritan "*Priscilla*," in a long gray cloak, and holding in her hand what the Germans call *Andachts-*

No. 427. *"The New Forest, from near Lymington: Afternoon."* THOMAS COLLIER, R.I.

No. 937. *"In Donington Park."* JAMES ORROCK.

No. 736. *"Kilchurn Castle, Loch Awe."* KEELEY HALSWELLE.

No. 223. *"A Sluice-Gate, Walberswick."* THOMAS PYNE.

such —a book of piety. Alas! the maiden herself by temperament is less pious, or, at all events, less austere than her guise. Like Mr. Abbey's heroines, she is Puritan more by

No. 848. *"A Shattered Veteran."* J. W. WHYMPER.

raiment than by blood. In her temperament there is the love of this life. But who shall say that her character is not natural? This beautiful little drawing hung, in the exhibition, almost on the spot where hung last year the president's greater design—the now famous *"Admonition."*

No. 1032. *"Yeldham Hall, Essex."* CHARLES EARLE, R. I.

Opposite to it, and, like it, almost in the center of a wall of the middle room, one saw what is almost, if it is not quite, the greatest of contemporary landscape-work in water-color —Mr. Thomas Collier's contribution, *"The New Forest."* The forest, as Mr. Collier loves it is not a mass of closely planted trees, but rather a stretch of upland and open country, with the heather upon it, and, down away in the hollow, a few writhing oak-trees and some squatters' cottages, and over all the passing clouds, gray and silvery, of a sky, of wind, and of shower. Mr. Thomas Collier is a man of middle age, who, in the eyes of those who understand art best, has reached the summit of his profession. He is one of the purest of water-color painters, and the seeming economy of his method is an economy that is sparing only of touches, and is never sparing of time. For in truth he is a slow worker.

No. **683.**   "*The Queen of the Night.*"   G. S. WALTERS.

He exhibits but few drawings, and the subjects of these are generally confined to the open country. If it is not a heath, it must be a flattish shore; it must be somewhere where the sky is wide and the air infinite.

Mr. Harry Hine is a landscape-painter, not less eminent than Mr. Collier. He is a veteran, and was already in manhood when David Cox and Peter Dewint were doing their best work. But his own labor, unlike that of Thomas Collier, betrays little of their influence. If he was influenced at all, he was influenced by Copley Fielding, whose subjects, like his own were subjects of Sussex—who, like Hine, was a painter of the Downs. Mr. Hine had six drawings in the gallery of the Institute this year, but none of them easily

No. 406. *"Funeral March of a Hero."* W. L. Wyllie.

No. 596. *"The Graces."* J. Fullenlove, R. I.

No. 275. *"Among the Missing: News in a Cornish Fishing Village."* WALTER LANGLEY.

No. 458. *"Tom Pinch and Ruth."* CHARLES GREEN.

reproduced in a sketch in black and white. One was a vision of the stormy sea, as unlike his habitual themes as was his *"Front of Old Brighton"* in the show of last season. He is fond of displaying variety and versatility. But it is upon the Downs—the chalk Downs of a golden September—that he is in truth most at home. *"Leaves from the London Road"* was his great Down-drawing this year. *"Evening"* and *"Dawn"* were also studies in the country that is most truly his. In his work all is harmony, unity of impression. The

No. 230. *"Encore."* G. G. KILBURNE.

objects represented are few. There are a flock of sheep, a shepherd, perhaps, a track over the grass, and a wind-bent thorn-tree; further, a turn and fold of the Downs, and an always placid and spacious sky.

Mr. Whymper and Mr. Keeley Halswelle are painters of a landscape that is more dramatic and more immediately striking; Mr. Mogford is picturesque, Mr. Orrock sturdy and downright; and the Institute has lately been joined by younger men—some of them painters in oil for the most part—who contribute to the variety and popularity of the exhibition. But many of these men—Mr. Colin Hunter is a type of them—are more properly discussed in the section devoted to the Royal Academy, where their most important labor makes its appearance. The Institute has several spirited painters of the sea, or of marine and river

No. 1073. "*The End of the Skating.*" TOWNELEY GREEN.

subjects. Mr. Hayes is one of the elder of these, and Mr. Wyllie one of the younger. Edwin Hayes has long been a painter of "dirty" weather, of a troubled sea in autumn, of luggers finding it hard to make for a port, and of bulky and weighty waters that might shatter feeble craft. The barge and the bargee are favorite themes of Mr. Wyllie's, and the waters of the Thames near London and the flat shores—the horizontal line broken here and there by the tall chimney of a cement-works. But a characteristic drawing, too, is that which is reproduced in the sketch, "*The Funeral March of a Hero*" (page 219). There is

No. **22.** "*The President of the Royal Institute of Painters in Water-Colors.*" T. WALTER WILSON, R. I.

little fault to find with it, but that it recalls too closely the famous Turner, "The Fighting Téméraire tugged to its Last Resting-place."

Generally speaking, it is a merit of Mr. Wyllie's to have discovered the picturesque elements in subjects we often deem commonplace. With that keen vision and firm hand of

No. 1081. *"A Diver."* WALTER CRANE.

No. 1071. *"He giveth his beloved sleep"* (*Psalm cxxvii, 2*). HENRY J. STOCK.

his he can make such subjects interesting; but of course he can never give them distinction and elegance. He is a painter of the work-a-day world. Now, a contemporary of his comparatively young—both men would seem to be between thirty and forty—is a painter, above all things, of subjects which are elegant and distinguished to begin with, but upon which his art of composition and his magic of color can bestow an added grace. This is Mr. John Fulleylove, whose *"Three Graces"* and *"The Dial"* are sufficiently characteristic examples of his drawings of quaint or stately gardens—Renaissance gardens in which the forms of nature are subdued to the service of art. He is the painter of the statue, the terrace, and the fountain; of the row of garden-lilies and of the clipped yew-trees. Such

No. 571. *"The Garland."* EDITH MARTINEAU.

work has the poetry, not indeed of passion any more than of simplicity, but at least of quietude and dignity. And Mr. Elgood, who is Mr. Fulleylove's kinsman, follows Mr. Fulleylove in the themes of his work. But his method is less severe; he condescends more to detail; he is more obviously pretty. The influence of the smaller designs of Frederick Walker, and of certain dainty labor of Mrs. Allingham, is perceptible.

A year or two ago Mr. Walter Langley, a young Birmingham artist, who had hardly before that time been heard of, sent to the Dudley Gallery in London some drawings of Cornish peasantry and fisher-folk which arrested much attention. Until just now, in the picture before us, Mr. Walter Langley has continued in the pursuit of the same theme; but this year he is more dramatic, and *"Among the Missing"* has made a distinct mark. It is one

29

of the merits of the picture that it tells its own story with directness and intelligibility. A crowd—they are all that are left at home in the fishing-village—gather round the post-office for news, after stormy weather, of those that put to sea. For some the news is reassuring—their friends will return—but the man who is dearest to this one in the foreground will never come back. The young wife, or the sweetheart, is led away by some elder companion, but the tempest of her grief has broken upon her.

The expression of passion lies perhaps at Mr. Walter Langley's command. Let us hope that he will exercise his gift with discretion as well as with sincerity, for English art has

No. 636. "*A Fairy Tale.*" G. A. Storey, A. R. A.

need of the presence of it. It is a gift that is hardly so much as sought for by several of the most accomplished of our figure-draughtsmen—by Mr. Charles Green, for instance, and Mr. E. J. Gregory. Charles Green, like William Small, is known best of all as an illustrator. The London illustrated newspapers owe much of their charm to these artists' designs. Charles Green draws correctly and with dainty expressiveness, and he has an almost unexampled command over the quaintest and sometimes the simplest types of English middle-class character. "*Tom Pinch and Ruth*" shows, I hope, to the reader of these

No. 679. *"Returning from Market, Connemara."* W. SMALL.

No. 570. *"Pigtails and Powder."* FRANK DADD, R. I.

lines something of his charm. But many of the designs of Mr. Green, exhibited from year to year at the Institute, are not illustrations at all, but are pure inventions. Like most artists of costumed figure, Mr. Green has a period which he particularly affects. He knows the whole of the eighteenth century, from the youth of Hogarth to the old age of Sir

No. 456. *"Faisant la Galette."* H. King.

Joshua. But the time that he has "invented," so to say—the time that he has brought into fashion—is that of the Directory and of the First Empire. He has an equal feeling for humor and for grace. His humor is never exaggerated, and his grace is never softened to effeminacy.

To turn to Mr. E. J. Gregory, my own view of him—and I have had the opportunity of expressing it at length in a recent article in "The Magazine of Art"—is that he is one of the very foremost of the artists of our day, and a man who has accepted his own time frankly and with heartiness. Like Mr. Wyllie, he is possessed by the charm of the actual. He calls nothing common nor unclean—hardly even does he call anything commonplace. He makes the commonplace interesting. And he is even modern of the moderns. He does not disdain the house-boat nor the tricycle, and the flounced modern figure lies beautifully for him in the garden hammock. This year the Institute shows three quite charming and widely varying works from his hand. One of them is a portrait of himself, called "*A Look at the Model.*" It is painted for Mr. C. J. Galloway, of Manchester, who is the fortunate owner of a whole gallery of Gregorys. Then there is the tricycle-drawing and the hammock-drawing. A very favorite little model of this artist's—Mr. Gregory's own sister-in-law—rides on the tricycle, in one, and, in the other, rests in the hammock. The hammock-drawing has the finish of a Meissonier; yet no one can be bolder than Mr. Gregory when he chooses. Gregory is very great in the arts of composition. He can see the artistic aspect of com-

No. 677. "*Captain Absolute and Lydia Languish.*" H. R. STEER.

monplace material, or just what it wants to give it charm. He has an extraordinary power of painting what he sees. The question of interest, as concerns his future, is, whether he will continue to paint (for the pleasure of those few who can appreciate them) the artistic aspects of modern life; or whether, at some moment in his career, he will see modern life rather from the dramatic than the purely artistic side, and so will paint a picture which shall compel the attention of the large public.

Mr. Kilburne—the author of the "*Encore*," sketched on page 221—is Mr. Gregory's senior by some ten or a dozen years, yet he is but a middle-aged man, and, if his work were generally or even often conceived in a modern spirit, one might expect very much from him still. I do not say he is old-fashioned, and I appreciate the daintiness of his execution and the delicacy of his sentiment. He paints, generally, the discreet "interiors" of the well-to-do or of the rich. But in an "*Encore*" he passes a little beyond his usual themes. The scene is, of course, a public concert, and Mr. Kilburne's heroine is before the world. The conception of the work shows the refinement and good taste of the agreeable artist to

No. 45. "*An Untidy Corner.*" Miss MARION CHASE.

whom it is due. And the drawing is very graceful. Yet Mr. E. J. Gregory certainly—and perhaps Mr. Henshall too—would have somehow found the occasion for displaying, in the treatment of that theme, a more learned art of composition. Like Mr. Henshall's somewhat kindred drawing at the gallery of the society—which I have already spoken of—the scale is unusually large for work in water-colors.

Another large and in some respects important drawing in the same room as Mr. Kilburne's—the first of the three rooms which the Institute employs—was Mr. Towneley Green's "*Good-by.*" Towneley Green is Charles Green's younger brother, and an artist of less marked individuality, of less piquant humor, than the painter of "*Tom Pinch and Ruth*," in the exhibition under notice, and of the yet more admirable "*Oranges, Apples, and*

No. 176. *"The Old Wellesley."* C. E. Holloway.

Bill o' the Play," of last year's show. But Towneley Green has nevertheless a quiet individuality of his own, and, if he is a less certain and a less subtile draughtsman than his
brother, he is at times a sweeter colorist. A good example of his style is shown in the

No. 925. *"Possession is Nine Points of the Law."* S. T. Dadd.

accompanying sketch (No. 1073, page 222). His other picture, "*A Good-by,*" depicts the
parting between guests and hostess at the gate of a country house.

Perhaps the last figure-picture of modern life which it is necessary to speak about is

Mr. Walter Wilson's portrait of the president in his studio (page 223). It is a present from the artist to the body of which he is a member, and is a most worthy and refined record of the painter whom it celebrates. The gesture is extremely characteristic, and the likeness excellent. The unobtrusiveness of the method of treatment is as memorable as the

No. 516. "*The Lord of the Glen.*" J. MacWhirter.

verisimilitude of the portrait. All is in a low key: the studio, with its little gallery, the suits of armor—for Mr. Linton is a connoisseur and a collector of armor—the gray tapestries, the easel, and the picture thereupon. It would have been very easy to make a drawing that would be more striking; but difficult, perhaps, to produce a portrait that would be more satisfactory.

No. 880. *"Highland Drovers resting after the Day's Journey."* John J. Richardson.

No. 648. *"Something wrong."* Thomas Huson.

A little group of painters belonging to the Institute—Mr. Walter Crane, Mr. Spencer Stanhope, and Mr. H. J. Stock, are among them—are faithful generally to the "ideal" and the symbolic. But Mr. Crane's "*A Diver*" is this year a frank vision of a nude male figure plunging into the transparent depths, and it is drawn with greater force and with greater spirit than Mr. Crane is apt to bestow on his habitually tender design. Mr. H. J. Stock

No. 248. "*Tour d'Horloge, Place de l'Hôtel de Ville, Auxerre.*" L. J. Wood.

exhibits four pictures, one of which we have sketched (No. 1071, page 224). In No. 399 he has engaged in the extraordinary task of attempting to realize with the brush and the sponge the following not very intelligible passage from the "*Sartor Resartus*": "Thus, in the conducting medium of Fantasy, flames forth that *fire*—development of the universal Spiritual Electricity—which, as unfolded between Man and Woman, we first emphatically denominate Love." There are those, no doubt, who can follow his interpretation of this obscure text. For me, the text and the interpretation are alike too elevated. I can not grasp, I can not attain unto them. Nor is the uncontrolled idealism of Mr. Spencer Stanhope—and his equally uncontrolled draughtsmanship—any more engaging. There is here, indeed, an amiable persistency in feebleness—a perseverance in unwarranted ambition—which ends only by irritating.

It seems a relief to pass from a presentation of unpresentable things to the Old-World grace of Mr. Abbey, as it was shown in "*A Bible-Reading.*" Never surely was there depicted, with more of tranquil humor, or with keener sense of the picturesque and the delicate, a Puritan household in which there is a mingling of the comely and the quaint. It is a pious exercise, but gloom by no means envelops the family circle. Mr. Abbey has but to acquire a more complete command of the resources of color to insure for the original drawing, as well as he may now insure for the black-and-white of the reproduction, a wide popularity for such design as this.

We need not mention in much detail the drawings of Mr. Small and Mr. Staniland, but their names can hardly be omitted. Mr. Staniland is very unequal. He is apt now to

No. 365. "*A Glimpse of the Clyde from above Helensburgh.*" ALFRED EAST.

attract and now to repel, and what would probably be accounted his most important contribution to this summer's exhibition of the Institute was a drawing in which the Gretchen of "Faust" was presented without refinement or poetry :

"*Bin weder Fräulein, weder schön,*
Kann ungeleitet nach Hause gehen"—

Gretchen says, undoubtedly, but she need not have been wanting in attractiveness because she was not a lady, nor in refinement because she did not reckon herself beautiful. Mr. Small, who, like Mr. Staniland, was not seen quite at his best, is a very successful illustrator. His illustrations have bestowed a momentary interest on more than one impossible story in the "Cornhill Magazine," and his designs for the *édition de luxe* of Fielding— whatever they have lacked—have shown fertility of resource and freedom of handling in watercolor.

Mr. Clausen, again, is another artist who has before now pleased us more thoroughly than during the present year. This year he has been, perhaps, a little deficient in individu-

No. 748. "*Waiting.*" C. J. Lewis.

ality. Mr. Bastien-Lepage has influenced him too much. But Mr. Clausen is dexterous, and he has feeling and subtilty; he is ingenious as a follower of other men's ways, but he is most interesting when he is himself.

Mr. Frank Dadd and Mr. Steer are young contributors; the one attracting attention by an almost audacious humor, in which somehow art has not been forgotten; and the other winning notice as a painter of the picturesque interior, as an artist alive to the charm of dignified line and of passing light. His "*Captain Absolute and Lydia Languish*" shows, moreover, a measure of the dramatic faculty, if he has invented quite all that he has portrayed. But the illustration of English classic drama—and Sheridan is a classic indeed!—may now gain much from the spectacle of the theatre, and, with the best intentions of originality, it is hardly possible to avoid deriving some inspiration from the ever-changing pictures which pass before the foot-lights. The actor is confessedly indebted to the painter for something of his knowledge of the outward aspects of the past world, and he repays the debt when the rapid succession of his significant gestures passes before the eye of the painter, making him acquainted with the aspect of emotions he can hardly profess to have experienced.

F. W.

No. 712. *"Days of my Girlhood."* Edith Berkley.

No. 785. *"Close of a Winter's Day."* D. C. WYLLIE.

INDEX TO ARTISTS.

ROYAL ACADEMY.

GROSVENOR GALLERY.

INSTITUTE OF PAINTERS IN OIL-COLORS.

31

THE WATER-COLOR SOCIETIES.

No. 215. "*Alice in Wonderland.*" Patrick W. Adam.

www.ingramcontent.com/pod-product-compliance
Lightning Source LLC
Chambersburg PA
CBHW031402270326
41929CB00010BA/1299